G000135458

# Contents

Italian borlotti bean, pumpkin & farro soup ...................................... 8

Strawberry cheesecakes .......................................................... 9

Spiced chickpea soup ............................................................ 9

Moroccan roast lamb with roasted roots & coriander ............................. 10

Asparagus & new potato frittata ................................................ 12

Cashew curry ................................................................... 12

Veggie kofta pittas with pick & mix sides ...................................... 14

Little spicy veggie pies ....................................................... 15

Best Yorkshire puddings ........................................................ 16

Coleslaw with tahini yogurt dressing ........................................... 18

Harissa-crumbed fish with lentils & peppers .................................... 18

Turkey minestrone .............................................................. 19

Hake & seafood cataplana ....................................................... 20

Lamb with buckwheat noodles & tomato dressing .................................. 21

Paneer jalfrezi with cumin rice ................................................ 22

Spicy tuna & cottage cheese jacket ............................................. 23

Tomato, onion & cucumber raita ................................................. 24

Low 'n' slow rib steak with Cuban mojo salsa ................................... 24

Herbed pork fillet with roast vegetables ....................................... 26

Charred broccoli, lemon & walnut pasta ......................................... 27

Chicken, chickpea & lemon casserole ............................................ 28

Chicken gumbo .................................................................. 28

Smoky chickpeas on toast ....................................................... 29

Frazzled chorizo & rocket linguine ............................................. 30

Pasta with chilli tomatoes & spinach ........................................... 31

Prawn sweet chilli noodle salad ................................................ 32

Pickled red onion & radish................................................................33

Baked asparagus risotto................................................................33

Chilli chicken wraps................................................................34

Pistachio nut & spiced apple Bircher muesli................................................................35

Broccoli pasta shells................................................................36

Chocolate sponge with hot chocolate custard................................................................37

Asparagus & lemon spaghetti with peas................................................................38

Mustardy greens................................................................39

Courgette, leek & goat's cheese soup................................................................39

Salmon salad with sesame dressing................................................................40

Mediterranean potato salad................................................................41

Potato, pea & egg curry rotis................................................................42

Easy chicken casserole................................................................43

Warm roasted squash and Puy lentil salad................................................................44

Tuna sweetcorn burgers................................................................45

Chicken & leek pies................................................................46

Mushroom, spinach & potato pie................................................................46

Harissa chicken with chickpea salad................................................................47

Spicy vegetable chapati wraps................................................................48

Spicy turkey & pepper bake................................................................49

Crab & sweetcorn chowder................................................................50

Fruitburst muffins................................................................51

Thai turkey stir-fry................................................................52

Spicy prawn noodle salad................................................................53

Avocado, labneh, roasted carrots & leaves................................................................54

Lighter apple & pear pie................................................................55

Haddock & spinach cheese melt................................................................56

Spiced cod with quinoa salad & mint chutney................................................................56

Smashed chicken with corn slaw ............................................................57

Fruity sponge cake ............................................................................59

Hearty mushroom soup .......................................................................60

Poached apricots with rosewater ............................................................61

Pan-fried rib-eye steak .......................................................................61

Moroccan-style chicken stew .................................................................62

Leek, tomato & barley risotto with pan-cooked cod ......................................63

Green minestrone with tortellini .............................................................64

Lighter moussaka with crunchy feta & oregano ...........................................65

Easy vegan pho ................................................................................66

Vegetable fried rice ...........................................................................67

Tomato & rice soup ...........................................................................67

Seared beef salad with capers & mint ......................................................68

Minty griddled chicken & peach salad ......................................................69

Artichoke, red onion & rosemary risotto ...................................................70

Easy tomato pizzas ...........................................................................71

Indian winter soup ............................................................................72

Quick banana ice cream ......................................................................74

Curried turkey lettuce wraps .................................................................74

Fruity coconut creams ........................................................................75

Mushroom & potato soup .....................................................................75

Sticky pork ....................................................................................76

Veggie okonomiyaki ..........................................................................77

Thai spiced turkey patties with noodle salad ..............................................78

Prawn chow mein .............................................................................79

Thai fried prawn & pineapple rice ...........................................................80

Feta & clementine lunch bowl ...............................................................81

Mushroom brunch ............................................................................81

Tuna, avocado & quinoa salad ........................................................................................82

Creamy linguine with ham, lemon & basil ........................................................................83

Steamed bass with pak choi ............................................................................................84

Sausage & butternut squash shells ..................................................................................84

Rhubarb & strawberry meringue pots ..............................................................................86

Miso mushroom & tofu noodle soup ................................................................................87

Mexican egg roll ..............................................................................................................87

Puy lentils with spinach & sour cherries ..........................................................................88

Tuna sweet potato jackets ................................................................................................88

New potato & tamarind salad ..........................................................................................89

Sesame salmon, purple sprouting broccoli & sweet potato mash ....................................90

Creamy smoked salmon, leek & potato soup ....................................................................91

Open leek & sweet potato pie ..........................................................................................92

Apple & sultana porridge ................................................................................................93

Chipotle chicken tacos with pineapple salsa ....................................................................94

Peach crumble ................................................................................................................95

Coriander cod with carrot pilaf ........................................................................................95

Ginger & lime chicken with sweet potato mash ................................................................96

Easy lentil curry ..............................................................................................................97

Curried aubergine & potato pie ........................................................................................98

Spinach & barley risotto ..................................................................................................99

Braised baby leeks ........................................................................................................100

Turkey & avocado toast ..................................................................................................101

Herb & garlic baked cod with romesco sauce & spinach ................................................101

Chicken with crispy Parma ham ....................................................................................102

Five-spice beef & sugar snap noodles ............................................................................103

Lemony salmon & lettuce wraps ....................................................................................104

Chicken & avocado sandwich topper ..............................................................................105

Raspberry chia jam ..................................................... 105

Thai-style fish broth with greens ...................................... 106

Pepper & lemon spaghetti with basil & pine nuts ........................ 107

Pasta with tuna & tomato sauce ......................................... 108

Oaty fish & prawn gratins .............................................. 108

Skinny chicken Caesar salad ............................................ 109

Chocolate chia pudding ................................................. 110

Leek, mushroom & goat's cheese strudels ................................ 111

Cabbage with caraway ................................................... 112

Lime prawn cocktail pitta salad ........................................ 112

Ham, mushroom & spinach frittata ....................................... 113

Crunchy detox salad .................................................... 114

Peach Melba smoothie ................................................... 115

Ham hock & cabbage hash ................................................ 115

Chicken & mushroom pancake topping ..................................... 116

Crisp chicken burgers with lemon mayo .................................. 117

Courgette lasagne ...................................................... 118

Pea & feta pearl barley stew ........................................... 119

Veggie olive wraps with mustard vinaigrette ............................ 120

Cucumber, pea & lettuce soup ........................................... 120

Mexican rice & bean salad .............................................. 121

Thin-stemmed broccoli with hoisin sauce & fried shallots ............... 122

Rich paprika seafood bowl .............................................. 123

One-pan prawn & tomato curry ........................................... 123

Easy Thai beef salad ................................................... 125

Penne with broccoli, lemon & anchovies ................................. 125

Walnut & almond muesli with grated apple ............................... 126

Lemony prawn pasta ..................................................... 127

Minced beef cobbler .................................................................................... 128

Tasty cottage pie with parsnip mash ............................................................ 129

Turkey & spring onion wraps ....................................................................... 130

Lighter chicken tacos ................................................................................... 130

Chicken & broccoli potato-topped pie .......................................................... 132

Chinese chicken noodle soup with peanut sauce ........................................... 134

Crab & lemon spaghetti with peas ............................................................... 135

Apple pie samosas ....................................................................................... 136

Banana pancakes ......................................................................................... 136

Green eggs ................................................................................................... 137

Roast pork with couscous & ginger yogurt .................................................. 138

Lamb & squash biryani with cucumber raita ............................................... 139

Roasted red pepper & tomato soup with ricotta .......................................... 140

Creamy yogurt porridge ............................................................................... 141

Noodles with turkey, green beans & hoisin ................................................. 142

Ginger & soy sea bass parcels ..................................................................... 143

Vegetarian bean pot with herby breadcrumbs ............................................. 144

Savoy cabbage with shallots & fennel seeds ............................................... 145

Healthy salad Niçoise ................................................................................... 145

Mumbai potato wraps with minted yogurt relish ......................................... 146

Banana & cinnamon pancakes with blueberry compote ............................... 147

15-minute chicken pasta ............................................................................... 148

Easy turkey paella ....................................................................................... 149

Teriyaki prawns & broccoli noodles ............................................................ 150

Spicy mince & lettuce cups ......................................................................... 150

Black-eyed bean mole with salsa ................................................................. 151

Avocado hummus & crudités ....................................................................... 152

Breakfast super-shake ................................................................................... 153

Avocado & strawberry ices ....................................................................................154

Salmon pasta salad with lemon & capers ............................................................154

Thai shredded chicken & runner bean salad ........................................................155

Squash & chorizo stew .........................................................................................156

Miso steak ...........................................................................................................157

Beef bulgogi stir-fry ............................................................................................158

Beetroot & butternut stew ...................................................................................159

Thai cucumber slaw .............................................................................................160

BBQ salad pizza ..................................................................................................161

Courgetti bolognese ............................................................................................162

Lighter aubergine Parmigiana .............................................................................163

Yogurt parfaits with crushed strawberries & amaretti ........................................165

Slow-cooker ham with sticky ginger glaze .........................................................165

Wild salmon with coconut chutney & green pilau ...............................................166

Bean, ham & egg salad ........................................................................................167

Lemony mushroom pilaf ......................................................................................168

Ultimate toad-in-the-hole with caramelised onion gravy ....................................169

Turkey burgers with beetroot relish ....................................................................170

Berry bake with passion fruit drizzle ..................................................................171

Prawn & pak choi stir-fry ....................................................................................172

Mushroom & chickpea burgers ...........................................................................173

Asian pulled chicken salad ..................................................................................174

Curtido .................................................................................................................175

Goat's cheese, tomato & olive triangles ..............................................................175

# Italian borlotti bean, pumpkin & farro soup

**Prep:**15 mins **Cook:**35 mins

**Serves 6**

## Ingredients

- 4 tbsp extra virgin olive oil , plus extra to serve
- 1 onion , finely chopped
- 1 celery stick , cut into chunks
- 750g pumpkin or squash, peeled, deseeded and cut into small chunks
- 1 carrot , peeled and cut into chunks
- 3 garlic cloves , chopped
- 3 tbsp tomato purée
- 1.2l chicken stock or vegetable stock
- 75g farro or mixed grains (such as barley or spelt)
- 50-80g parmesan rinds or vegetarian alternative (optional), plus a few shavings to serve
- 400g can borlotti beans , drained
- 2 handfuls baby spinach
- 2 tbsp chopped parsley or 8 whole sage leaves

**Method**

**STEP 1**

Heat the oil in a heavy-bottomed saucepan. Add the onion, celery, pumpkin or squash and carrot and cook until the vegetables have some colour. Add a splash of water and some seasoning, then cover the pan and let the vegetables cook over a very low heat for 5 mins.

**STEP 2**

Add the garlic and cook for another couple of mins, then add the tomato purée, stock, mixed grains, parmesan rinds, if using, and some seasoning. Simmer for about 15 mins (or until the grains are cooked), adding the beans for the final 5 mins. In the last few mins, add the spinach, then taste for seasoning.

**STEP 3**

If you want to use sage, fry the leaves whole in a little olive oil before adding to the soup. If you prefer to use parsley, you can just add it directly to the soup. Serve with shavings of parmesan and a drizzle of extra virgin olive oil on top of each bowlful. Remove the parmesan rinds and serve.

# Strawberry cheesecakes

**Prep:**10 mins **Serves 4**

# Ingredients

- 85g low-fat biscuit (we used WeightWatchers ginger biscuits)
- 200g tub extra-light soft cheese
- 200g tub 0% fat Greek yogurt
- 4 tbsp caster sugar
- few drops vanilla extract
- 2 tbsp good-quality strawberry jam
- 100g strawberry , hulled and sliced

**Method**

**STEP 1**

Put the biscuits in a plastic bag and bash with a rolling pin until you have chunky crumbs. Divide between 4 glasses or small bowls.

**STEP 2**

Beat the soft cheese, yogurt, sugar and vanilla together until smooth, then spoon over the crumbs and chill until you are ready to serve.

**STEP 3**

Stir the jam in a bowl until loose, then gently stir in the strawberries. Divide the strawberries between the cheesecakes and serve.

# Spiced chickpea soup

**Prep:**10 mins **Cook:**25 mins

**Serves 4**

## Ingredients

- 1 tbsp olive oil
- 1 onion , chopped
- 2 garlic cloves , crushed
- 1 red chilli , deseeded and roughly chopped
- 1 tbsp grated fresh ginger
- 1 tsp cumin
- 1 tsp ras-el-hanout
- ¼ tsp cinnamon
- 200g roasted red pepper , from a jar
- 2 x 400g cans chopped tomato
- 400ml vegetable stock
- 400g can chickpea , drained and rinsed
- 2 preserved lemons , rind chopped (discard the pulp and seeds)
- 1 tbsp clear honey
- 50g wholewheat couscous

## Method

### STEP 1

Heat the oil in a large lidded pan. Add the onion and garlic, put on the lid and cook for 5 mins, stirring halfway through. Stir the chilli, ginger, cumin, ras el hanout and cinnamon into the pan and cook for 1 min. Add the peppers, tomatoes and stock. Bring to the boil, turn down to a simmer, put on the lid and cook for 10 mins.

### STEP 2

Blitz the soup with a stick blender, or in a food processor until smooth. Return to the pan and add more liquid to thin the soup, if you like. Stir in the chickpeas, preserved lemons, honey and some seasoning. If eating straight away, add the couscous and heat through for 5 mins. (If taking to work, add the couscous just before reheating).

# Moroccan roast lamb with roasted roots & coriander

**Prep:**15 mins **Cook:**55 mins

Serves 4

# Ingredients

- ½ leg of lamb , around 800g
- 2 red onions , cut into wedges
- 1 butternut squash , skin left on, cut into wedges
- 1 celeriac , peeled and cut into wedges
- 2½ tbsp cold pressed rapeseed oil
- 2 tbsp ras el hanout
- 8 garlic cloves , skin on
- 1 small bunch coriander
- ½ tsp cumin seeds
- 1 lemon , zested and juiced
- 1/2 green chilli , deseeded

**Method**

## STEP 1

Take the lamb out of the fridge while you chop the onions, squash and celeriac. Heat oven to 200C/180C fan/gas 6. Trim any excess fat off the leg of lamb, then cut a few slashes into the meat. Rub ½ tbsp oil and 1 tbsp ras el hanout over the lamb and season with salt and pepper. Put the onion, celeriac, butternut squash into a large roasting tin with the garlic. Toss with the remaining ras el hanout, remaining oil and some salt and pepper. Nestle the lamb into the tin and put in the oven to roast for 40 mins.

## STEP 2

Take the lamb out of the oven and leave to rest. Put the veg back in the oven for 20 mins. Meanwhile, blitz the coriander, cumin seeds, lemon zest, lemon juice and green chilli together in a mini food processor until finely chopped and vivid green.

## STEP 3

Carve the lamb, put on a platter, then pile on the veg. Sprinkle over some of the coriander mixture before taking the platter to the table for everyone to help themselves.

# Asparagus & new potato frittata

**Prep:**10 mins **Cook:**12 mins

**Serves 3**

## Ingredients

- 200g new potatoes, quartered
- 100g asparagus tips
- 1 tbsp olive oil
- 1 onion, finely chopped
- 6 eggs, beaten
- 40g cheddar, grated
- rocket or mixed leaves, to serve

**Method**

**STEP 1**

Heat the grill to high. Put the potatoes in a pan of cold salted water and bring to the boil. Once boiling, cook for 4-5 mins until nearly tender, then add the asparagus for a final 1 min. Drain.

**STEP 2**

Meanwhile, heat the oil in an ovenproof frying pan and add the onion. Cook for about 8 mins until softened.

**STEP 3**

Mix the eggs with half the cheese in a jug and season well. Pour over the onion in the pan, then scatter over the asparagus and potatoes. Top with the remaining cheese and put under the grill for 5 mins or until golden and cooked through. Cut into wedges and serve from the pan with salad.

# Cashew curry

**Prep:**20 mins **Cook:**1 hr

**Serves 3**

# Ingredients

- 1 small onion , chopped
- 3-4 garlic cloves
- thumb-sized piece ginger , peeled and roughly chopped
- 3 green chillies , deseeded
- small pack coriander , leaves picked and stalk roughly chopped
- 100g unsalted cashews
- 2 tbsp coconut oil
- 1 ½ tbsp garam masala
- 400g can chopped tomatoes
- 450ml chicken stock
- 3 large chicken breasts (about 475g), any visible fat removed, chopped into chunks
- 155g fat-free Greek yogurt
- 10ml single cream (optional)

## To serve

- 165g boiled or steamed greens (choose from spinach, kale, runner beans, asparagus or broccoli)

## Method

## STEP 1

Put the onion, garlic, ginger, chillies and coriander stalks in a small food processor and blitz to a paste.

## STEP 2

Heat a large, non-stick frying pan over a medium heat. Add the cashews and toast for 1-2 mins until light golden. Set aside and return the pan to the heat. Add the oil and stir-fry the paste for 5 mins to soften. Add the garam masala and cook for a further 2 mins.

## STEP 3

Add the tomatoes and stock to the pan. Mix well, then tip into a blender with the cashews and blitz until smooth. Return to the pan, season and bring to the boil, then lower to a simmer.

## STEP 4

Cook for 30 mins until the sauce has thickened then add the chicken, cover with a lid and simmer for another 15 mins, until the chicken is cooked through. Add the yogurt and cream (if using), and stir well to make a creamy sauce.

**STEP 5**

Scatter with the coriander leaves and serve with the greens.

# Veggie kofta pittas with pick & mix sides

**Prep:**20 mins **Cook:**30 mins

**Serves 6**

## Ingredients

- 2 onions , chopped
- 2 garlic cloves , crushed
- 1 Cal cooking spray , for frying
- 2 x 400g cans chickpeas , drained
- 100g fresh brown breadcrumbs
- 1 large egg
- 2 tsp ground cumin
- 2 tsp ground coriander
- zest 1 lemon , 1 tbsp juice, plus extra wedges to serve
- 85g baby spinach
- toasted pitta breads , to serve
- 175g fat-free natural or Greek yogurt , to serve
- pickled chillies or jalapeños (optional), to serve

**For the carrot & tomato salad**

- 200g carrots , coarsely grated
- 200g tomatoes , diced
- ½ red onion , finely chopped
- 2 tbsp red wine vinegar

- 1 tsp sugar

**Method**

## STEP 1

Soften the onions and garlic with a few sprays of 1 Cal cooking spray and a splash of water in a non-stick pan. Once really soft, tip into a food processor with the chickpeas, breadcrumbs, egg, spices, lemon zest and juice, and plenty of seasoning. Pulse until fairly smooth, then add 30g of the spinach and pulse until finely chopped. Shape the mixture into 12 sausage-shaped koftas and put on a baking-parchment-lined baking tray. Chill while you heat oven to 200C/180C fan/gas 6.

## STEP 2

Spray the koftas a few times more with cooking spray, then bake for 20-25 mins until crisp and golden.

## STEP 3

Meanwhile, mix together all the carrot salad ingredients with some seasoning. Put the remaining spinach in a bowl and warm the pittas following pack instructions.

## STEP 4

Serve the koftas with warm pittas, extra spinach, carrot salad, fat-free yogurt and pickled chillies, if you like.

# Little spicy veggie pies

**Prep:**10 mins **Cook:**55 mins

**Serves 4**

# Ingredients

- 2 tbsp rapeseed oil
- 2 tbsp finely chopped ginger
- 3 tbsp Korma curry powder
- 3 large garlic cloves , grated
- 2 x 400g cans chickpeas , undrained
- 320g carrots , coarsely grated

- 160g frozen sweetcorn
- 1 tbsp vegetable bouillon powder
- 4 tbsp tomato purée
- 250g bag spinach , cooked

**For the topping**

- 750g potatoes , peeled and cut into 3cm chunks
- 1 tsp ground coriander
- 10g fresh coriander , chopped
- 150g coconut yogurt

**Method**

**STEP 1**

To make the topping, boil the potatoes for 15-20 mins until tender then drain, reserving the water, and mash with the ground and fresh coriander and yogurt until creamy.

**STEP 2**

While the potatoes are boiling, heat the oil in a large pan, add the ginger and fry briefly, tip in the curry powder and garlic, stirring quickly as you don't want it to burn, then tip in a can of chickpeas with the water from the can. Stir well, then mash in the pan to smash them up a bit, then tip in the second can of chickpeas, again with the water from the can, along with the carrots, corn, bouillon and tomato purée. Simmer for 5-10 mins, adding some of the potato water, if needed, to loosen.

**STEP 3**

Heat the oven to 200C/180C fan/gas 6. Spoon the filling into four individual pie dishes (each about 10cm wide, 8cm deep) and top with the mash, smoothing it to seal round the edges of the dishes. If you're following our Healthy Diet Plan, bake two for 25 mins until golden, and cook half the spinach, saving the rest of the bag for another day. Cover and chill the remaining two pies to eat another day. Will keep in the fridge for four days. If freezing, to reheat, bake from frozen for 40-45 mins until golden and piping hot.

# Best Yorkshire puddings

**Prep:**5 mins **Cook:**20 mins

**Makes 8 large puds or 24 small**

**Ingredients**

- 140g plain flour (this is about 200ml/7fl oz)
- 4 eggs (200ml/7fl oz)
- 200ml milk
- sunflower oil , for cooking

**Method**

**STEP 1**

Heat oven to 230C/fan 210C/gas 8.

**STEP 2**

Drizzle a little sunflower oil evenly into two 4-hole Yorkshire pudding tins or two 12-hole non-stick muffin tins and place in the oven to heat through.

**STEP 3**

To make the batter, tip 140g plain flour into a bowl and beat in 4 eggs until smooth.

**STEP 4**

Gradually add 200ml milk and carry on beating until the mix is completely lump-free. Season with salt and pepper.

**STEP 5**

Pour the batter into a jug, then remove the hot tins from the oven. Carefully and evenly pour the batter into the holes.

**STEP 6**

Place the tins back in the oven and leave undisturbed for 20-25 mins until the puddings have puffed up and browned.

**STEP 7**

Serve immediately. You can now cool them and freeze for up to 1 month.

# Coleslaw with tahini yogurt dressing

**Prep:** 15 mins No cook

**Serves 6**

## Ingredients

- 1 ½ tbsp tahini paste
- 5 tbsp Greek-style natural yogurt
- ½ garlic clove , crushed
- 1 small red cabbage , quartered and finely sliced
- 3 small carrots , cut into fine matchsticks
- 1 small onion , halved and finely sliced

**Method**

**STEP 1**

Put the tahini, yogurt, garlic, and some seasoning in a large bowl and mix until smooth. The dressing will thicken so add 2-3 tbsps cold water to loosen it. Add the vegetables to the dressing, and toss together until everything is well coated.

# Harissa-crumbed fish with lentils & peppers

**Prep:** 15 mins **Cook:** 15 mins

**Serves 4**

## Ingredients

- 2 x 200g pouches cooked puy lentils
- 200g jar roasted red peppers , drained and torn into chunks
- 50g black olives , from a jar, roughly chopped
- 1 lemon , zested and cut into wedges
- 3 tbsp olive or rapeseed oil
- 4 x 140g cod fillets (or another white fish)

- 100g fresh breadcrumbs
- 1 tbsp harissa
- ½ small pack flat-leaf parsley , chopped

**Method**

**STEP 1**

Heat oven to 200C/180C fan/gas 6. Mix the lentils, peppers, olives, lemon zest, 2 tbsp oil and some seasoning in a roasting tin. Top with the fish fillets. Mix the breadcrumbs, harissa and the remaining oil and put a few spoonfuls on top of each piece of fish. Bake for 12-15 mins until the fish is cooked, the topping is crispy and the lentils are hot. Scatter with the parsley and squeeze over the lemon wedges.

# Turkey minestrone

**Prep:** 15 mins **Cook:** 40 mins

**Serves 6**

# Ingredients

- 2 tsp olive oil
- 100g smoked bacon lardons
- 1 red onion , finely chopped
- 1 carrot , finely chopped
- 1 celery stick , finely chopped
- 2 garlic cloves , finely chopped
- 2 bay leaves
- 2 thyme sprigs
- 300g celeriac (or any other root veg), cut into cubes
- 200g potato , cut into cubes
- 400g can borlotti beans , drained and rinsed
- 1 ½l chicken stock or turkey stock, (fresh is best)
- 350g cooked turkey
- 100g orzo
- 75g curly kale , shredded

**Method**

## STEP 1

Heat 1 tsp of oil in a large saucepan. Add the bacon and fry over a medium-to-high heat for 4-5 mins or until golden, then set aside.

## STEP 2

Put the remaining oil, the onion, carrot, celery and a pinch of salt in the pan. Cook gently over a low heat for 8-10 mins, stirring occasionally, until the veg is soft but not coloured. Add the garlic and herbs, and cook for 2 mins more

## STEP 3

Tip in the celeriac, potato, borlotti beans and chicken stock. Bring to the boil, then simmer, uncovered, for 10-15 mins. Add the cooked turkey, orzo and the bacon, and cook for 10 mins.

## STEP 4

Just before serving, tip in the kale, give everything a good stir and return to the heat for about 2 mins or until the kale has wilted.

# Hake & seafood cataplana

**Prep:**15 mins **Cook:**35 mins

**Serves 2**

## Ingredients

- 2 tbsp cold-pressed rapeseed oil
- 1 onion , halved and thinly sliced
- 250g salad potatoes , cut into chunks
- 1 large red pepper , deseeded and chopped
- 1 courgette (200g), thickly sliced
- 2 tomatoes , chopped (150g)
- 2 large garlic cloves , finely grated
- 1 tbsp cider vinegar (optional)
- 2 tsp vegetable bouillon powder
- 2 skinless hake fillets (pack size 240g)
- 150g pack ready-cooked mussels (not in shells)
- 60g peeled prawns

- large handful of parsley , chopped

**Method**

**STEP 1**

Heat the oil in a wide non-stick pan with a tight-fitting lid. Fry the onions and potatoes for about 5 mins, or until starting to soften. Add the peppers, courgettes, tomatoes and garlic, then stir in the vinegar, if using, the bouillon and 200ml water. Bring to a simmer, cover and cook for 25 mins, or until the peppers and courgettes are very tender (if your pan doesn't have a tight-fitting lid, wet a sheet of baking parchment and place over the stew before covering – this helps keep in the juices).

**STEP 2**

Add the hake fillets, mussels and prawns, then cover and cook for 5 mins more, or until the fish flakes easily when tested with a fork. Scatter over the parsley and serve.

# Lamb with buckwheat noodles & tomato dressing

**Prep:** 15 mins **Cook:** 25 mins

**Serves 2**

# Ingredients

- 12 cherry tomatoes , quartered
- 1 tsp fish sauce
- juice and zest 1 lime
- 1 tbsp sweet chilli sauce
- 100g buckwheat noodle
- 2 tsp rapeseed oil
- 1 red onion , halved and sliced
- 1 carrot , cut into matchsticks
- 1 red pepper , deseeded and sliced
- 100g shredded white cabbage
- 200g lean lamb loin fillet or steaks, diced
- 4 tbsp chopped fresh mint

**Method**

### STEP 1

Lightly squash the tomatoes with the fish sauce, lime juice and zest, and the chilli sauce. Cook the noodles following pack instructions.

### STEP 2

Meanwhile, heat the oil in a wok and stir-fry the onion, carrot and pepper for 5 mins or until softening. Add the cabbage and cook for a few mins more. Remove the vegetables from the pan, add the lamb and cook for 5-8 mins so that it is still tender and juicy. Take the pan off the heat, toss in the noodles, vegetables, tomato dressing and mint, and serve.

# Paneer jalfrezi with cumin rice

**Prep:**20 mins **Cook:**30 mins

**Serves 4**

## Ingredients

- 2 tsp cold-pressed rapeseed oil
- 1 large and 1 medium onion , large one finely chopped and medium one cut into wedges
- 2 large garlic cloves , chopped
- 50g ginger , peeled and shredded
- 2 tsp ground coriander
- 2 tsp cumin seeds
- 400g can chopped tomatoes
- 1 tbsp vegetable bouillon powder
- 135g paneer , chopped
- 2 large peppers , seeded and chopped
- 1 red or green chilli , deseeded and sliced
- 25g coriander , chopped

**For the rice**

- 260g brown basmati rice
- 1 tsp cumin seeds

**Method**

**STEP 1**

Heat 1 tsp oil a large non-stick frying pan and fry the chopped onions, garlic and half the ginger for 5 mins until softened. Add the ground coriander and cumin seeds and cook for 1 min more, then tip in the tomatoes, half a can of water and the bouillon. Blitz everything together with a stick blender until very smooth, then bring to a simmer. Cover and cook for 15 mins.

## STEP 2

Meanwhile, cook the rice and cumin seeds in a pan of boiling water for 25 mins, or until tender.

## STEP 3

Heat the remaining oil in a non-stick wok and fry the paneer until lightly coloured. Remove from the pan and set aside. Add the peppers, onion wedges and chilli to the pan and stir-fry until the veg is tender, but still retains some bite. Mix the stir-fried veg and paneer into the sauce with the chopped coriander, then serve with the rice. If you're following our Healthy Diet Plan, eat two portions of the curry and rice, then chill the rest for another day. Will keep for up to three days, covered, in the fridge. To serve on the second night, reheat the leftover portions in the microwave until piping hot.

# Spicy tuna & cottage cheese jacket

**Prep:** 10 mins **Cook:** 1 hr

**Serves 1**

# Ingredients

- 225g can tuna , drained
- ½ red chilli , chopped
- 1 spring onion , sliced
- handful halved cherry tomatoes
- ½ small bunch coriander , chopped
- 1 medium-sized jacket potato
- 150g low-fat cottage cheese

**Method**

**STEP 1**

Preheat the oven to 180C/Gas 4/fan oven 160C. Prick the potato several times with a fork and put it straight onto a shelf in the hottest part of the oven. Bake for approximately 1 hour, or until it is soft inside.

**STEP 2**

Mix tuna with chilli, spring onion, cherry tomatoes and coriander. Split jacket potato and fill with the tuna mix and cottage cheese.

# Tomato, onion & cucumber raita

**Prep:**10 mins **Cook:**5 mins

**Serves 8**

# Ingredients

- 1 ripe tomato , chopped into 1cm dice
- ¼ red onion , finely chopped
- 85g cucumber , finely chopped
- a large handful chopped coriander
- 1 tsp cumin seeds , toasted and coarsely ground
- 450g plain yogurt , whisked until smooth
- sugar , to taste

**Method**

**STEP 1**

Stir together the tomato, red onion, cucumber, coriander, cumin seeds, plain yogurt, and a large pinch of sugar. Season to taste, adding more sugar if it is particularly sour.

# Low 'n' slow rib steak with Cuban mojo salsa

**Prep:**20 mins **Cook:**3 hrs and 20 mins

**Serves 2**

# Ingredients

- 1 rib steak on the bone or côte du boeuf (about 800g)

- 1 tbsp rapeseed oil
- 1 garlic clove
- 2 thyme sprigs
- 25g butter , chopped into small pieces
- sweet potato fries
- a dressed salad , to serve

## For the mojo salsa

- 2 limes
- 1 small orange
- ½ small bunch mint , finely chopped
- small bunch coriander , finely chopped
- 4 spring onions , finely chopped
- 1 small garlic clove , crushed
- 1 fat green chilli , finely chopped
- 4 tbsp extra virgin rapeseed oil or olive oil

## Method

### STEP 1

Leave the beef at room temperature for about 1 hr before you cook it. Heat oven to 60C/40C fan/gas 1 /4 if you like your beef medium rare, or 65C/45C fan/gas 1 /4 for medium. (Cooking at these low temperatures will be more accurate in an electric oven than in a gas one. If using gas, put the oven on the lowest setting you have, and be aware that the cooking time may be shorter.)

### STEP 2

Put the unseasoned beef in a heavy-based ovenproof frying pan. Cook in the middle of the oven for 3 hrs undisturbed.

### STEP 3

Meanwhile, make the salsa. Zest the limes and orange into a bowl. Cut each in half and place, cut-side down, in a hot pan. Cook for a few mins until the fruits are charred, then squeeze the juice into the bowl. Add the other ingredients and season well.

### STEP 4

When the beef is cooked, it should look dry on the surface, and dark pink in colour. If you have a meat thermometer, test the internal temperature – it should be 58-60C. Remove the pan from the oven and set over a high heat on the hob. Add the oil and sear the meat on both sides for a few mins until caramelised. Sear the fat for a few mins too. Smash the garlic clove with the heel of your hand and add this to the pan with the thyme and butter. When the butter is foaming, spoon it over the beef and cook for another 1-2 mins. Transfer the beef to a warm plate, cover with foil, and leave to rest for 5-10 mins. Carve away from the bone and into slices before serving with the salsa, fries and salad.

# Herbed pork fillet with roast vegetables

**Total time** 1 hr and 45 mins Takes around 1½ - 1¾ hours

**Serves 4**

## Ingredients

- 4 medium parsnips, peeled and quartered lengthways
- 1 butternut squash (about 650g/1lb 7oz), peeled, seeded and cut into chunks
- 2 red onions, each cut into 8 wedges
- 1 tbsp olive oil
- grated zest of 1 lemon
- 2 tsp pork seasoning or dried mixed Italian herbs
- 500g lean pork tenderloin, in one or two pieces
- 1 medium Bramley apple
- 400ml hot chicken stock

**Method**

**STEP 1**

Preheat the oven to 200C/ gas 6/fan 180C. Put all the vegetables into a roasting tin. Drizzle with the olive oil, season with salt and pepper, then toss everything together.

**STEP 2**

On a plate, mix together the lemon zest and pork seasoning or herbs. Roll the pork tenderloin in the mixture, then put it on top of the vegetables. Roast for 40 minutes.

**STEP 3**

Peel and core the apple and cut it into chunks. Scatter the pieces into the roasting tin, then pour in the hot stock and cook for a further 15-20 minutes. Slice the pork, arrange on a platter with the veg, then spoon the pan juices on top.

# Charred broccoli, lemon & walnut pasta

**Prep:** 5 mins **Cook:** 15 mins

**Serves 2**

# Ingredients

- 1 head broccoli , cut into small florets and stalk cut into small pieces
- 3 tsp olive oil
- 150g penne or fusilli
- 2 garlic cloves , crushed
- 1 tbsp roughly chopped walnuts
- pinch of chilli flakes
- ½ lemon , zested and juiced

**Method**

**STEP 1**

Heat the grill to high. Put the broccoli on a baking tray and drizzle over 1 tsp of the oil. Season, and toss together. Grill for 8-10 mins, tossing around halfway through, until crispy and charred.

**STEP 2**

Cook the pasta in salted water following pack instructions. Drain, reserving a cup of the cooking water.

**STEP 3**

In a frying pan, heat the remaining 2 tsp oil over a medium heat, and fry the garlic, walnuts and chilli for 3-4 mins until golden.

**STEP 4**

Tip in the pasta, broccoli, lemon zest and juice, reserving a little of the zest. Add a splash of the reserved cooking water and toss everything together to coat the pasta. Serve in warmed bowls with the remaining lemon zest scattered over.

# Chicken, chickpea & lemon casserole

**Total time**40 mins Ready in 35-40 minutes

**Serves 2**

## Ingredients

- 175g new potato , halved (Charlotte would work well)
- 1 medium onion , thinly sliced
- 2 slices lemon , chopped
- 2 garlic cloves , roughly chopped
- 1 tsp ground cumin
- 1 tsp ground cinnamon
- 450ml chicken stock
- large skinless, boneless chicken thighs , trimmed of all fat and cut into cubes
- ½ x can chickpea
- handful fresh coriander , chopped

**Method**

**STEP 1**

Put the potatoes, onion, lemon and garlic into a casserole or heavy saucepan. Sprinkle over the ground spices and season lightly. Toss together then pour over the stock. Bring to the boil and simmer for 12 mins or until potatoes are tender.

**STEP 2**

Add the chicken and chickpeas, cover the saucepan and simmer gently for a further 10-12 mins or until the chicken is cooked through. Check the seasoning and stir in the coriander. Serve with steamed green beans or broccoli.

# Chicken gumbo

**Prep:**25 mins **Cook:**35 mins

**Serves 4**

## Ingredients

- 1 tbsp olive oil
- 500g skinless, boneless chicken thigh , cut into chunks
- 1 onion , chopped
- 1 green pepper , deseeded and chopped
- 3 celery sticks, finely chopped
- 1 garlic clove , finely chopped
- ¼ tsp cayenne pepper
- 1 tsp smoked paprika
- 1 tsp ground cumin
- 1 tsp dried thyme
- 1 bay leaf
- 1 heaped tbsp plain flour
- 400g can chopped tomato
- 400ml chicken stock
- 100g okra , cut into 2cm rounds
- small handful sage , leaves chopped
- crusty bread or microwave rice, to serve

**Method**

**STEP 1**

Heat the oil in a large pan over a medium high heat. Add the chicken and cook in batches for about 5 mins to brown all over. Remove the chicken with a slotted spoon and set aside.

**STEP 2**

Add the onion, green pepper and celery to the pan, put on the lid and cook for 5 mins, stirring occasionally until softened a little. Stir in the garlic, spices, thyme and bay leaf and cook for 1 min until fragrant. Return the chicken and any juices to the pan with the flour, stirring to coat everything. Pour in the tomatoes and stock, and bring to the boil, cook for 5 mins, then add the okra and half the sage. Turn down to a simmer, put on the lid and cook for 10 mins. Then season and serve, scattering the rest of the sage over.

# Smoky chickpeas on toast

**Prep:**2 mins **Cook:**10 mins

**Serves 2**

## Ingredients

- 1 tsp olive oil or vegetable oil, plus a drizzle
- 1 small onion or banana shallot, chopped
- 2 tsp chipotle paste
- 250ml passata
- 400g can chickpeas , drained
- 2 tsp honey
- 2 tsp red wine vinegar
- 2-4 slices good crusty bread
- 2 eggs

**Method**

**STEP 1**

Heat ½ tsp of the oil in a pan. Tip in the onion and cook until soft, about 5-8 mins, then add the chipotle paste, passata, chickpeas, honey and vinegar. Season and bubble for 5 mins.

**STEP 2**

Toast the bread. Heat the remaining oil in a frying pan and fry the eggs. Drizzle the toast with a little oil, then top with the chickpeas and fried eggs.

# Frazzled chorizo & rocket linguine

**Prep:**5 mins **Cook:**15 mins

**Serves 2**

# Ingredients

- 140g linguine
- 4 small cooking chorizo, cut into small chunks
- 2 tbsp capers, drained
- juice 1 lemon
- 50g bag rocket

**Method**

**STEP 1**

Cook the linguine following pack instructions. Meanwhile, put the chorizo in a cold frying pan over a low heat, then gradually increase it. Enough oil will be released by the chorizo to brown it without adding extra.

## STEP 2

Stir and fry the chorizo until it is completely frazzled, then lift it out onto a plate.

## STEP 3

Add the capers to the frying pan and cook for 1 min. Scoop them out and discard any excess oil.

## STEP 4

Drain the pasta and add the chorizo and capers along with the lemon juice and rocket. Season and toss everything together.

# Pasta with chilli tomatoes & spinach

**Prep:**10 mins **Cook:**20 mins

**Serves 2**

# Ingredients

- 2 tsp olive oil
- 1 onion , finely chopped
- 2 garlic cloves , crushed
- ½ tsp dried chilli flakes
- 200g wholemeal penne pasta
- 400g can chopped tomato
- 100ml red wine
- ½ tsp dried oregano
- 125g bag young spinach leaves
- 25g parmesan or vegetarian alternative, grated

**Method**

## STEP 1

Heat the oil in a non-stick frying pan and gently fry the onion, garlic and chilli flakes, stirring regularly, for 5 mins (add a little water if they begin to stick).

**STEP 2**

Cook pasta following pack instructions. Add the tomatoes, wine and oregano to the frying pan and stir to combine. Bring to a gentle simmer and cook, stirring occasionally, for 10 mins.

**STEP 3**

Shake the spinach into the pan and cook for 1-2 mins until wilted. Drain the pasta and tip into the pan with the sauce. Toss to combine, sprinkle with cheese and serve.

# Prawn sweet chilli noodle salad

**Prep:**10 mins **Cook:**5 mins

**Serves 4 - 6**

## Ingredients

- 3 nests medium egg noodles
- ½ large cucumber
- bunch spring onions , finely sliced
- 100g cherry tomato , halved
- 1 green chilli , deseeded, finely chopped
- 200g cooked king prawns , defrosted if frozen
- zest and juice 2 limes
- 4 tbsp sweet chilli sauce
- 100g baby spinach leaves
- 25g roasted cashew

**Method**

**STEP 1**

Boil the noodles for 4 mins, then drain. Cool under running water, then drain again. Put into a large bowl, then using scissors, cut into shorter lengths.

**STEP 2**

Halve cucumber lengthways, then scoop out the seeds. Slice into halfmoons and add to the noodles with the onions, tomatoes, chilli and prawns.

**STEP 3**

Mix the lime zest, juice and chilli sauce to make a dressing and fold through noodles. Put a handful of spinach onto each serving plate, top with the noodles and cashews.

# Pickled red onion & radish

**Prep:** 10 mins **Cook:** 2 mins plus resting

**Serves 6**

## Ingredients

- 1 large red onion
- 12 small radishes
- 1 tbsp golden caster sugar
- 100ml cider vinegar

**Method**

**STEP 1**

Slice 1 large red onion into thin rings and 12 small radishes into thin slices. Stir in 1 tbsp salt and 1 tbsp golden caster sugar and leave for 20 mins. Warm 100ml cider vinegar and 50ml water in a small saucepan, then pour over the vegetables. Stir to dissolve the sugar and salt, then leave to cool.

# Baked asparagus risotto

**Prep:** 10 mins **Cook:** 45 mins

**Serves 4**

## Ingredients

- 2 tsp olive oil
- 1 small onion , chopped
- 300g risotto rice
- 400ml can asparagus soup
- 850ml vegetable stock
- small bunch parsley , chopped
- 300g asparagus , ends trimmed

- 10 cherry tomatoes , halved
- 25g parmesan (or vegetarian alternative), grated

## Method

### STEP 1

Heat oven to 200C/180C fan/gas 6. Heat the oil in an ovenproof casserole dish, add the onion and cook for 5 mins until softened. Add the rice and cook for 1 min more, stirring to coat in the oil. Tip in the soup and stock, season and stir well to combine, then bring to the boil. Cover and place in the oven.

### STEP 2

Bake for 15 mins, then remove the dish from the oven, give the rice a good mix, stirring in the parsley. Place the asparagus and tomatoes on top of the rice. Return to the oven, uncovered, for a further 15 mins. Scatter with the cheese to serve.

# Chilli chicken wraps

**Prep:**10 mins **Cook:**25 mins

**Serves 4**

## Ingredients

- 2 tbsp vegetable oil
- 6 boneless, skinless chicken thighs, cut into bite-sized pieces
- 1 large onion, thinly sliced into half-moons
- 2 garlic cloves, finely chopped
- 3cm piece ginger, peeled and finely chopped
- ½ tsp ground cumin
- ½ tsp garam masala
- 1 tbsp tomato purée
- 1 red chilli, thinly sliced into rings
- juice ½ lemon
- 4 rotis, warmed
- ½ small red onion, chopped
- 4 tbsp mango chutney or lime pickle
- 4 handfuls mint or coriander

- 4 tbsp yogurt

**Method**

**STEP 1**

Heat the oil in a large frying pan over a medium heat. Add the chicken, brown on all sides, then remove. Add the onion, garlic, ginger and a pinch of salt. Cook for 5 mins or until softened.

**STEP 2**

Increase the heat to high. Return the chicken to the pan with the spices, tomato purée, chilli and lemon juice. Season well and cook for 10 mins or until the chicken is tender.

**STEP 3**

Divide the chicken, red onion, chutney, herbs and yogurt between the four warm rotis. Roll up and serve with plenty of napkins

# Pistachio nut & spiced apple Bircher muesli

**Prep:** 10 mins plus overnight soaking, no cook

**Serves 2**

# Ingredients

**For the base ingredients**

- 50g jumbo porridge oat
- 50ml apple juice
- large pinch cinnamon
- large pinch nutmeg
- 1 medium apple , cored and grated
- 2 tbsp low-fat natural yogurt

**For the topping**

- 25g chopped pistachio
- 3 tbsp pomegranate seeds or mixed berries

**Method**

## STEP 1

Mix all the base ingredients, except the yogurt, with 150ml water and leave to soak for at least 20 mins or overnight, if possible. Once the oats have softened, stir through the yogurt, then divide the mixture between 2 bowls. Sprinkle half of the topping over each bowl and serve.

# Broccoli pasta shells

**Prep:**5 mins **Cook:**15 mins

**Serves 4**

# Ingredients

- 1 head of broccoli, chopped into florets
- 1 garlic clove, unpeeled
- 2 tbsp olive oil
- 250g pasta shells
- ½ small pack parsley
- ½ small pack basil
- 30g toasted pine nuts
- ½ lemon, zested and juiced
- 30g parmesan (or vegetarian alternative), plus extra to serve

**Method**

**STEP 1**

Heat the oven to 200C/180C fan/gas 6. Toss the broccoli and garlic in 1 tbsp of the olive oil on a roasting tray and roast in the oven for 10-12 mins, until softened.

**STEP 2**

Tip the pasta shells into a pan of boiling, salted water. Cook according to packet instructions and drain. Tip the parsley, basil, pine nuts, lemon juice and parmesan into a blender. Once the broccoli is done, set aside a few of the smaller pieces. Squeeze the garlic from its skin, add to the blender along with the rest of the broccoli, pulse to a pesto and season well.

**STEP 3**

Toss the pasta with the pesto. Add the reserved broccoli florets, split between two bowls and top with a little extra parmesan, the lemon zest and a good grinding of black pepper, if you like.

# Chocolate sponge with hot chocolate custard

**Prep:**30 mins **Cook:**40 mins plus soaking

**Serves 12**

## Ingredients

⅓rd of a portion

- 300g stoned date , chopped            100gm
- 6 large eggs , separated                  2 eggs
- 350g light muscovado sugar           100gm — to mucu with dates.
- 200g wholemeal flour                     66gm
- 2 tsp baking powder                        ½tsp baking powder
- 100g cocoa                                        30gm.

### For the custard

- 5 tbsp custard powder
- 5 tbsp light muscovado sugar
- 50g cocoa powder
- 1.2l skimmed milk

**Method**

**STEP 1**

Cover the dates with boiling water and set aside to soften for 30 mins.

**STEP 2**

Heat oven to 160C/140C fan/gas 3 and line a 20 x 30cm baking tin with baking parchment. Drain the dates, reserving the liquid, then whizz the dates to a purée with 100ml of the soaking liquid.

**STEP 3**

Beat the egg whites in a large bowl with an electric whisk until stiff peaks hold on the end of your whisk. Add half the sugar and beat until thick and glossy.

## STEP 4

In another bowl, beat the yolks and remaining sugar until pale. Whisk in the mashed date mixture, then fold into the egg white mixture until well combined. Mix the flour, baking powder and cocoa with a pinch of salt. Sprinkle over the wet mixture and very gently fold in until well combined. Gently scrape into the tin and spread to the edges. Bake for 35-40 mins until a skewer poked in comes out clean.

## STEP 5

Meanwhile, mix the custard powder, sugar and cocoa together in a saucepan. Stir in dribbles of milk until you get a smooth paste. Gradually add more milk until it's all incorporated with no lumps. Put over a medium heat and warm, stirring constantly, until thick and just bubbling.

## STEP 6

Cut the warm cake into slabs and pour over the hot chocolate custard to serve.

# Asparagus & lemon spaghetti with peas

**Prep:**7 mins **Cook:**12 mins

**Serves 2**

# Ingredients

- 150g wholemeal spaghetti
- 160g asparagus, ends trimmed and cut into lengths
- 2 tbsp rapeseed oil
- 2 leeks (220g), cut into lengths, then thin strips
- 1 red chilli, deseeded and finely chopped
- 1 garlic clove, finely grated
- 160g frozen peas
- 1 lemon, zested and juiced, plus wedges to serve

**Method**

**STEP 1**

Boil the spaghetti for 12 mins until al dente, adding the asparagus for the last 3 mins. Meanwhile, heat the oil in a large non-stick frying pan, add the leeks and chilli and cook for 5 mins. Stir in the garlic, peas and lemon zest and juice and cook for a few mins more.

**STEP 2**

Drain and add the pasta to the pan with ¼ mug of the pasta water and toss everything together until well mixed. Spoon into shallow bowls and serve with lemon wedges for squeezing over, if you like.

# Mustardy greens

**Prep:**10 mins **Cook:**5 mins

**Serves 4**

# Ingredients

- 300g spring green
- 300g frozen pea
- 25g butter
- 1 tbsp wholegrain mustard
- 2 tbsp Dijon mustard

**Method**

**STEP 1**

Heat 250ml water in a large pan. Add the greens and peas, cover with a lid and boil for 4 mins. Drain into a colander, put the pan back on the heat, and add the butter and mustards. When the butter has melted, add the veg back to the pan, season well and toss everything together. Serve straight away.

# Courgette, leek & goat's cheese soup

**Prep:**8 mins **Cook:**17 mins

**Serves 4**

## Ingredients

- 1 tbsp rapeseed oil
- 400g leeks, well washed and sliced
- 450g courgettes, sliced
- 3 tsp vegetable bouillon powder, made up to 1 litre with boiling water
- 400g spinach
- 150g tub soft vegetarian goat's cheese
- 15g basil, plus a few leaves to serve
- 8 tsp omega seed mix (see tip)
- 4 x 25g portions wholegrain rye bread

**Method**

**STEP 1**

Heat the oil in a large pan and fry the leeks for a few mins to soften. Add the courgettes, then cover the pan and cook for 5 mins more. Pour in the stock, cover and cook for about 7 mins.

**STEP 2**

Add the spinach, then cover the pan and cook for 5 mins so that it wilts. Take off the heat and blitz until really smooth with a hand blender. Add the goat's cheese and basil, then blitz again.

**STEP 3**

If you're making this recipe as part of our two-person Summer Healthy Diet Plan, spoon half the soup into two bowls or large flasks, then cool and chill the remainder for another day. Reheat in a pan or microwave to serve. If serving in bowls, scatter with some extra basil leaves and the seeds, and eat with the rye bread.

# Salmon salad with sesame dressing

**Prep:**7 mins **Cook:**16 mins

**Serves 2**

## Ingredients

**For the salad**

- 250g new potatoes , sliced
- 160g French beans , trimmed
- 2 wild salmon fillets
- 80g salad leaves
- 4 small clementines , 3 sliced, 1 juiced
- handful of basil , chopped
- handful of coriander , chopped

**For the dressing**

- 2 tsp sesame oil
- 2 tsp tamari
- ½ lemon , juiced
- 1 red chilli , deseeded and chopped
- 2 tbsp finely chopped onion (1/4 small onion)

**Method**

**STEP 1**

Steam the potatoes and beans in a steamer basket set over a pan of boiling water for 8 mins. Arrange the salmon fillets on top and steam for a further 6-8 mins, or until the salmon flakes easily when tested with a fork.

**STEP 2**

Meanwhile, mix the dressing ingredients together along with the clementine juice. If eating straightaway, divide the salad leaves between two plates and top with the warm potatoes and beans and the clementine slices. Arrange the salmon fillets on top, scatter over the herbs and spoon over the dressing. If taking to work, prepare the potatoes, beans and salmon the night before, then pack into a rigid airtight container with the salad leaves kept separate. Put the salad elements together and dress just before eating to prevent the leaves from wilting.

# Mediterranean potato salad

**Prep:**10 mins **Cook:**25 mins

**Serves 4**

# Ingredients

- 1 tbsp olive oil
- 1 small onion , thinly sliced
- 1 garlic clove , crushed
- 1 tsp oregano , fresh or dried
- ½ x 400g can cherry tomatoes
- 100g roasted red pepper , from a jar, sliced
- 300g new potato , halved if large
- 25g black olive , sliced
- handful basil leaves , torn

## Method

### STEP 1

Heat the oil in a saucepan, add the onion and cook for 5-10 mins until soft. Add the garlic and oregano and cook for 1 min. Add the tomatoes and peppers, season well and simmer gently for 10 mins.

### STEP 2

Meanwhile, cook the potatoes in a pan of boiling salted water for 10-15 mins until tender. Drain well, mix with the sauce and serve warm, sprinkled with olives and basil.

# Potato, pea & egg curry rotis

**Prep:**5 mins **Cook:**25 mins

**Serves 4**

## Ingredients

- 1 tbsp oil
- 2 tbsp mild curry paste
- 400g can chopped tomatoes

- 2 potatoes , cut into small chunks
- 200g peas
- 3 eggs , hard-boiled
- pack rotis , warmed through
- 150g tub natural yogurt , to serve

## Method

### STEP 1

Heat the oil in a saucepan and briefly fry the curry paste. Tip in the tomatoes and half a can of water and bring to a simmer. Add the potatoes and cook for 20 mins, or until the potato is tender. Stir in the peas and cook for 3 mins.

### STEP 2

Halve the eggs and place them on top of the curry, then warm everything through. Serve with the rotis and yogurt on the side.

# Easy chicken casserole

**Prep:**20 mins **Cook:**1 hr

**Serves 4**

## Ingredients

- 2 tbsp sunflower oil
- 400g boneless, skinless chicken thigh , trimmed and cut into chunks
- 1 onion , finely chopped
- 3 carrots , finely chopped
- 3 celery sticks, finely chopped
- 2 thyme sprigs or ½ tsp dried
- 1 bay leaf , fresh or dried
- 600ml vegetable or chicken stock
- 2 x 400g / 14oz cans haricot beans , drained
- chopped parsley , to serve

## Method

### STEP 1

Heat the oil in a large pan, add the chicken, then fry until lightly browned. Add the veg, then fry for a few mins more. Stir in the herbs and stock. Bring to the boil. Stir well, reduce the heat, then cover and cook for 40 mins, until the chicken is tender.

## STEP 2

Stir the beans into the pan, then simmer for 5 mins. Stir in the parsley and serve with crusty bread.

# Warm roasted squash and Puy lentil salad

**Prep:**10 mins **Cook:**30 mins

**Serves 4**

# Ingredients

- 1kg butternut squash , chunkily diced
- 1 ½ tbsp olive oil
- 1 garlic clove , crushed
- 2 tsp thyme leaves
- 1 tbsp balsamic vinegar
- 1 tsp wholegrain mustard
- x cans Puy lentils in water
- ½ red onion sliced
- 100g bag spinach
- 150g cherry tomatoes , halved
- 40g Cheshire cheese
- 1-2 tbsp toasted pumpkin seeds

**Method**

## STEP 1

Heat oven to 200C/180C fan/gas 4. Toss the butternut squash with 1 tbsp olive oil, garlic clove, thyme leaves and seasoning. Roast for 25-30 mins or until tender.

## STEP 2

Mix together the balsamic vinegar, ½ tbsp olive oil, the wholegrain mustard and 1-2 tbsp water. Drain the Puy lentils in water and toss with the dressing, red onion, spinach and cherry tomatoes.

## STEP 3

Divide the lentils between four plates. Top with the squash, then crumble over Cheshire cheese and pumpkin seeds.

# Tuna sweetcorn burgers

**Prep:**5 mins **Cook:**10 mins

**Serves 4**

# Ingredients

- 85g white bread , torn into pieces
- 198g can sweetcorn , drained
- 2 x cans tuna in water, drained well
- 25g grated cheddar
- 3 spring onions , finely chopped
- 1 egg , beaten
- 2 tbsp vegetable oil
- wholegrain bread rolls, lettuce, salsa, to serve

**Method**

**STEP 1**

Whizz the bread in a food processor to crumbs, tip into a bowl, then whizz half the sweetcorn until finely chopped. Add the chopped corn, remaining whole corn, tuna, cheese, spring onions and some seasoning into the bowl with the bread and mix well. Add the egg, bit by bit (you may not need it all), until the mixture is sticky enough to be shaped into four even-size burgers.

**STEP 2**

Heat the oil in a non-stick pan, then cook the burgers for 5 mins on each side until golden and hot through the middle. Stuff into wholemeal buns with your favourite lettuce and a good dollop of salsa.

# Chicken & leek pies

**Prep:**15 mins **Cook:**40 mins

**Serves 2**

## Ingredients

- 1 large sweet potato , cut into chunky chips
- 4 tsp olive oil
- 2 chicken breasts , chopped into bite-size chunks
- 1 leek , finely sliced
- 1 carrot , chopped
- 225ml low-sodium chicken stock
- 2 tsp wholegrain mustard
- 85g light soft cheese
- 2 tbsp chopped tarragon leaves
- 2 sheets filo pastry

**Method**

**STEP 1**

Heat oven to 200C/180C fan/gas 6. In a roasting tray toss the sweet potatoes with 2 tsp of the oil and some seasoning. Cook for 30-40 mins, until golden and crisp. Heat 1 tsp oil in a medium frying pan. Fry the chicken until browned, remove from the pan and set aside. Add the leek and a splash of water, and gently fry until soft, about 7 mins. Add the carrot and cook for 3 mins more. Pour in the stock and boil until reduced by half, then add the mustard and soft cheese, stirring well to combine. Return the chicken to the pan, add the tarragon and some seasoning.

**STEP 2**

Divide the mixture between 2 small ovenproof dishes. Take the filo sheets and scrunch them up. Top each pie with a sheet and brush with remaining 1 tsp oil. Cook the pies in the oven with the chips for 15 mins, until the pastry is golden.

# Mushroom, spinach & potato pie

**Prep:**15 mins **Cook:**45 mins

**Serves 4**

# Ingredients

- 400g baby spinach
- 1 tbsp olive oil
- 500g mushroom , such as chestnut, shiitake and button
- 2 garlic cloves , crushed
- 250ml vegetable stock (made from half a low sodium vegetable stock cube)
- 300g cooked new potatoes , cut into bite-sized pieces
- 1 tbsp grain mustard
- 1 tsp freshly grated nutmeg
- 2 heaped tbsp light crème fraîche
- 3 sheets filo pastry
- 300g each green beans and broccoli, steamed

**Method**

**STEP 1**

Heat oven to 200C/180C fan/gas 6. Wilt spinach in a colander by pouring a kettleful of hot water over it.

**STEP 2**

Heat half the oil in a large non-stick pan and fry mushrooms on a high heat until golden. Add garlic and cook for 1 min, then tip in stock, mustard, nutmeg and potatoes. Bubble for a few mins until reduced. Season, then remove from the heat; add crème fraîche and spinach. Pour into a pie dish and allow to cool for a few mins.

**STEP 3**

Brush filo with remaining oil, quarter sheets then loosely scrunch up and lay on top of pie filling. Bake for 20-25 mins until golden. Serve with vegetables.

# Harissa chicken with chickpea salad

**Prep:**15 mins **Cook:**8 mins

**Serves 2**

## Ingredients

- 250g punnet cherry tomatoes , halved
- ½ small red onion , chopped
- 400g can chickpeas , drained
- small bunch parsley , roughly chopped
- juice 1 lemon
- 2 skinless chicken breasts , halved lengthways through the middle
- 1 tbsp harissa
- fat-free natural yogurt and wholemeal pitta bread, to serve

**Method**

**STEP 1**

Mix the tomatoes, onion and chickpeas together, stir through the parsley and lemon juice and season.

**STEP 2**

Coat the chicken with the harissa. Heat a griddle or frying pan or barbecue. Cook the chicken for 3-4 mins each side until lightly charred and cooked through.

**STEP 3**

Divide the salad between 2 plates, top with the harissa chicken and serve with a dollop of yogurt and warmed pitta bread.

# Spicy vegetable chapati wraps

**Prep:**10 mins **Cook:**20 mins Ready in 20-30 minutes

**Serves 2**

## Ingredients

- 150g sweet potato , peeled and roughly cubed
- 200g can peeled plum tomatoes
- 200g can chickpeas , drained
- ½ tsp dried chilli flakes
- 1 tbsp mild curry paste

- 50g baby spinach leaves
- 1 tbsp chopped, fresh coriander
- 2 plain chapatis (Indian flatbreads)
- 2 tbsp fat-free Greek or natural yogurt

**Method**

**STEP 1**

Cook the sweet potatoes in a pan of boiling water for 10-12 minutes until tender. Meanwhile, put the tomatoes, chickpeas, chilli flakes and curry paste in another pan and simmer gently for about 5 minutes.

**STEP 2**

Preheat the grill. Drain the sweet potatoes and add to the tomato mixture. Stir in the spinach and cook for a minute until just starting to wilt. Stir in the coriander, season to taste and keep warm.

**STEP 3**

Sprinkle the chapatis with a little water and grill for 20-30 seconds each side. Spoon on the filling, top with yogurt and fold in half to serve.

# Spicy turkey & pepper bake

**Prep:**15 mins **Cook:**45 mins

Serves 4

# Ingredients

- 1kg potatoes , chopped
- 25g butter
- 300g frozen pepper
- 1 onion , chopped
- 500g pack turkey mince
- 1 red chilli , deseeded and chopped
- 1 tbsp smoked paprika
- 200ml hot chicken stock

**Method**

## STEP 1

Heat oven to 200C/180C fan/gas 6. Cook the potatoes in a large pan of salted water for 12-15 mins or until tender. Drain well, then return to the pan and allow to steam for 3 mins. Add some seasoning and the butter, then roughly mash with a fork and set aside until later.

## STEP 2

Meanwhile, cook the peppers and onion in a large pan for 5 mins – the water in the peppers should stop them sticking. Stir in the turkey mince, chilli and paprika and cook until browned. Pour in the stock, then bubble for 10 mins until thickened. Transfer the turkey mince into an ovenproof dish, top with the mash and cook for 30 mins or until golden and bubbling.

# Crab & sweetcorn chowder

**Prep:** 5 mins **Cook:** 30 mins

**Serves 4**

# Ingredients

- 1 onion , finely chopped
- 1 leek , green and white parts separated and sliced
- 2 carrots , chopped
- 850ml-1 litre/1.5 pints - 1.75 pints low-sodium chicken or vegetable stock
- 1 large potato , diced
- 175g/ 6oz frozen sweetcorn
- 170g can white crabmeat , drained
- 4 tbsp light crème fraîche
- 1 tsp chopped chives

**Method**

## STEP 1

Put the onion, white part of the leek and carrots in a large pan and pour on a few tbsp of the stock. Cook over a medium heat for about 10 mins, stirring regularly until soft. Add a splash more stock if the vegetables start to stick.

## STEP 2

Add the potato, green leek and most of the stock, and simmer for 10-15 mins, until the potato is tender. Tip in the sweetcorn and crab meat, then cook for a further 1-2 mins. Remove from the heat and stir in the crème fraîche and some seasoning. Add the rest of the stock if the soup is too thick. Sprinkle with the chives and serve with brown bread, if you like.

# Fruitburst muffins

**Prep:**20 mins - 25 mins **Cook:**20 mins - 25 mins Takes 40-50 minutes

**12 muffins**

# Ingredients

- 225g plain flour
- 2 tsp baking powder
- 2 large eggs
- 50g butter , melted
- 175ml skimmed milk
- 100ml clear honey
- 140g fresh blueberry
- 85g dried cranberry
- 140g seedless raisin
- 140g dried apricot , chopped
- 1 tsp grated orange zest
- 1 tsp ground cinnamon

**Method**

**STEP 1**

Preheat the oven to 200C/gas 6/ fan 180C and very lightly butter a 12-hole muffin tin. Sift the flour and baking powder into a bowl. In another bowl, lightly beat the eggs, then stir in the melted butter, milk and honey. Add to the flour with the remaining ingredients. Combine quickly without overworking (it's fine if there are some lumps left – you want it gloopy rather than fluid). Spoon the mixture into the muffin tin. Bake for 20-25 minutes until well risen and pale golden on top.

**STEP 2**

Leave in the tin for a few minutes before turning out. When cool, they'll keep in an airtight tin for two days. (Can be frozen for up to 1 month.)

# Thai turkey stir-fry

**Prep:**10 mins **Cook:**15 mins

**Serves 4**

## Ingredients

- 300g rice noodles
- 1 tsp sunflower oil
- 400g turkey breast steak , cut into thin strips and any fat removed
- 340g green beans , trimmed and halved
- 1 red onion , sliced
- 2 garlic cloves , sliced
- juice 1 lime , plus extra wedges for serving
- 1 tsp chilli powder
- 1 red chilli , finely chopped
- 1 tbsp fish sauce
- handful mint , roughly chopped
- handful coriander , roughly chopped

**Method**

**STEP 1**

Cook the rice noodles following pack instructions. Heat the oil in a non-stick pan and fry the turkey over a high heat for 2 mins. Add the beans, onion and garlic, and cook for a further 5 mins.

**STEP 2**

Stir in the lime juice, chilli powder, fresh chilli and fish sauce, then cook for 3 mins more. Stir in the noodles and herbs, then toss everything together before serving.

# Spicy prawn noodle salad

**Prep:** 15 mins **Cook:** 5 mins

**Serves 4**

# Ingredients

- 200g glass noodles (available from thai-food-online.co.uk) or rice vermicelli
- 1 tbsp vegetable oil
- 3 spring onions , sliced
- 2 lemongrass stalks , sliced
- 300g raw jumbo king prawns
- small handful mint
- small handful coriander
- small handful Thai basil
- ½ cucumber , cut into matchsticks

**For the dressing**

- 1 red bird's-eye chilli , roughly chopped
- 2 garlic cloves
- 2 limes , juiced
- 2 tbsp fish sauce
- 1 tsp soft brown sugar or palm sugar

**Method**

**STEP 1**

Cook the noodles following pack instructions. Drain, rinse with cold water and set aside.

**STEP 2**

Heat the oil in a frying pan over a medium heat and cook the spring onions and lemongrass for 2 mins or until softened. Add the prawns and cook for 3 mins or until they have turned pink. Tip everything into a large bowl and allow to cool while you make the dressing.

**STEP 3**

Put all the dressing ingredients in a mini chopper and blitz until very finely chopped. Taste and add a little more sugar (to sweeten) and fish sauce (to make saltier), if you like. Tip the noodles into the bowl with the prawns, then add the rest of the ingredients and dressing, and toss really well before serving.

# Avocado, labneh, roasted carrots & leaves

**Prep:**20 mins **Cook:**30 mins plus overnight chilling

**Serves 2**

# Ingredients

- 200g full-fat bio yoghurt
- grated zest 1 lime , plus 1 tbsp juice, cut into wedges, to serve
- 1/2 small pack coriander leaves, finely chopped
- 300g carrots , cut into batons
- 1 tbsp cold-pressed rapeseed oil
- 1/2 tsp ground cumin
- 1 ripe but firm avocado
- 50g bag mixed salad leaves
- 1 tbsp mixed seeds (such as sunflower, pumpkin, sesame and linseed)

**Method**

**STEP 1**

To make the labneh, mix the yoghurt, lime and coriander together in a bowl. Line another small bowl with a square of muslin. Spoon the yogurt mixture into the bowl, pull up the ends of the muslin and tie the yoghurt into a ball. Tie the ends of the muslin onto a wooden spoon and suspend over a bowl or jug. Place in the fridge overnight to strain.

**STEP 2**

Heat oven to 200C/180C fan/gas 6. Toss the carrots with 1 tsp of the oil, 2 tsp of the lime juice, the cumin and lots of ground black pepper. Tip onto a foil-lined baking tray and roast for 20 mins. Turn the carrots and return to the oven for a further 10 mins or until tender and lightly browned. Set aside.

**STEP 3**

Cut the avocado in half and remove the stone. Scoop out the flesh from each half in one piece with a serving spoon. Slice on a chopping board, then toss with the remaining lime juice.

## STEP 4

Untie the labneh and spread it over two plates, top with the salad leaves, carrots and avocado. Drizzle over the remaining oil, sprinkle with the seeds and serve with lime wedges.

# Lighter apple & pear pie

**Prep:**20 mins **Cook:**40 mins - 45 mins

**Serves 6**

# Ingredients

- 6 eating apples (we used Braeburn)
- 4 ripe pears
- zest and juice 1 lemon
- 3 tbsp agave syrup
- 1 tsp mixed spice
- 1 tbsp cornflour
- 4 filo pastry sheets
- 4 tsp rapeseed oil
- 25g flaked almond

**To serve**

- custard (made with custard powder and skimmed milk), fat-free Greek yogurt or low-fat frozen vanilla yogurt

**Method**

## STEP 1

Peel, core, and chop the apples and pears into large pieces, and throw into a big saucepan with the lemon juice, agave syrup, mixed spice and 200ml water. Bring to a simmer with the lid on, then take off the lid and cook, stirring, for about 5 mins until the apple is softening. Use a slotted spoon to scoop out three-quarters of the fruit chunks and put into a pie dish.

## STEP 2

Cover and cook the remaining fruit for another 4-5 mins until soft, then mash with a potato masher. Mix 1 tbsp of this with the cornflour to a smooth paste, then add back to the pan and bring back to a simmer, stirring, to thicken the sauce. Pour over the fruit in the pie dish and stir together. Heat oven to 180C/160C fan/gas 4.

### STEP 3

Lay out your sheets of filo and brush all over with oil – 1 tsp should be enough for 1 sheet. Scatter over the almonds and press to stick to the pastry, then crumple up each sheet as you lift it on top of the fruit. Bake for 20-25 mins until the pastry is browned and crisp. Serve straight away.

# Haddock & spinach cheese melt

**Prep:**5 mins **Cook:**25 mins

**Serves 2**

## Ingredients

- 200g baby spinach
- 85g low-fat soft cheese
- 2 x 140g/5oz pieces skinless haddock
- 1 large tomato , sliced
- 2 tbsp grated parmesan

**Method**

### STEP 1

Heat oven to 200C/180C fan/gas 6. Pile the spinach into a large pan over a medium heat, turning it over and over until wilted. Remove from the heat and drain off the excess liquid.

### STEP 2

Mix spinach with the soft cheese, then place in the bottom of a small baking dish and sit haddock pieces on top. Lay sliced tomatoes on top of the fish and sprinkle with the Parmesan. Bake for 15-20 mins (depending on thickness of the haddock), or until the fish flakes easily.

# Spiced cod with quinoa salad & mint chutney

**Prep:** 5 mins **Cook:** 25 mins

**Serves 2**

# Ingredients

- 40g quinoa (or 85g pre-cooked quinoa)
- 3 tbsp chopped mint
- 3 tbsp chopped coriander
- 150g pot 0% natural yogurt
- 1 garlic clove
- ¼ tsp turmeric
- pinch of cumin seeds
- 2 x 150g chunky fillets skinless white fish , such as sustainable cod
- ¼ cucumber , finely diced
- 1 small red onion , finely chopped
- 4 tomatoes , chopped
- good squeeze of lemon juice

**Method**

**STEP 1**

Tip the quinoa (if not pre-cooked) into a pan, cover with water and boil, covered, for 25 mins, checking the water level to make sure it doesn't boil dry. Drain well.

**STEP 2**

Meanwhile, put 2 tbsp each of the mint and coriander in a bowl. Add the yogurt and garlic, and blitz with a hand blender until smooth. Stir 2 tbsp of the herby yogurt with the turmeric and cumin, then add the fish and turn in the mixture to completely coat.

**STEP 3**

Turn the grill to High. Arrange the fish in a shallow heatproof dish and grill for 8-10 mins, depending on thickness, until it flakes. Toss the quinoa with the cucumber, onion, tomatoes, lemon juice and remaining herbs. Spoon onto a plate, add the fish and spoon round the mint chutney, or add it at the table.

# Smashed chicken with corn slaw

**Prep:**10 mins **Cook:**5 mins

**Serves 4**

# Ingredients

### For the chicken

- 4 skinless chicken breast fillets
- 1 lime , zested and juiced
- 2 tbsp bio yogurt
- 1 tsp fresh thyme leaves
- ¼ tsp turmeric
- 2 tbsp finely chopped coriander
- 1 garlic clove , finely grated
- 1 tsp rapeseed oil

### For the slaw

- 1 small avocado
- 1 lime , zested and juiced
- 2 tbsp bio yogurt
- 2 tbsp finely chopped coriander
- 160g corn , cut from 2 cobs
- 1 red pepper , deseeded and chopped
- 1 red onion , halved and finely sliced
- 320g white cabbage , finely sliced
- 150g new potatoes , boiled, to serve

### Method

### STEP 1

Cut the chicken breasts in half, then put them between two sheets of baking parchment and bash with a rolling pin to flatten. Mix the lime zest and juice with the yogurt, thyme, turmeric, coriander and garlic in a large bowl. Add the chicken and stir until well coated. Leave to marinate while you make the slaw.

### STEP 2

Mash the avocado with the lime juice and zest, 2 tbsp yogurt and the coriander. Stir in the corn, red pepper, onion and cabbage.

**STEP 3**

Heat a large non-stick frying pan or griddle pan, then cook the chicken in batches for a few mins each side – they'll cook quickly as they're thin. Serve the hot chicken with the slaw and the new potatoes. If you're cooking for two, chill half the chicken and slaw for lunch another day (eat within two days).

# Fruity sponge cake

**Prep:**10 mins **Cook:**20 mins

**Serves 8**

# Ingredients

- butter or oil, for greasing
- 50g plain flour
- 3 tbsp cornflour
- 1 tsp baking powder
- 4 eggs , separated
- 175g caster sugar

**For the filling**

- 295g can mandarin segment , drained
- 200g tub low-fat fromage frais
- icing sugar , for dusting

**Method**

**STEP 1**

Heat oven to 180C/fan 160C/gas 4. Grease then line the base and sides of 2 x 20cm sandwich tins with greaseproof paper. Sieve the flours and baking powder together.

**STEP 2**

Use electric hand beaters to whisk the egg whites until stiff, then briefly whisk in the sugar. Beat the egg yolks quickly, then whisk into the whites. Fold in the dry ingredients using a large metal spoon, then spoon the mixture into the tins and level the tops. Bake for 18-20 mins until risen, light golden and a skewer inserted into the middle comes out clean. Cool in the tins for 10 mins, then gently remove and leave to cool completely.

## STEP 3

Mix the mandarins and fromage frais together. Peel away the greaseproof paper, sandwich the cakes with the mandarin mix, then dust with the icing sugar to serve. Best eaten on the day it's made.

# Hearty mushroom soup

**Prep:**30 mins **Cook:**30 mins

**Serves 4 - 6**

# Ingredients

- 25g pack porcini mushrooms
- 2 tbsp olive oil
- 1 medium onion , finely diced
- 2 large carrots , diced
- 2 garlic cloves , finely chopped
- 1 tbsp chopped rosemary , or 1 tsp dried
- 500g fresh mushroom , such as chestnut, finely chopped
- 1.2l vegetable stock (from a cube is fine)
- 5 tbsp marsala or dry sherry
- 2 tbsp tomato purée
- 100g pearl barley
- grated fresh parmesan , to serve (optional)

**Method**

## STEP 1

Put the porcini in a bowl with 250ml boiling water and leave to soak for 25 mins. Heat the oil in a pan and add the onion, carrot, garlic, rosemary and seasoning. Fry for 5 mins on a medium heat until softened. Drain the porcini, saving the liquid, and finely chop. Tip into the pan with the fresh mushrooms. Fry for another 5 mins, then add the stock, marsala or sherry, tomato purée, barley and strained porcini liquid.

**STEP 2**

Cook for 30 mins or until barley is soft, adding more liquid if it becomes too thick. Serve in bowls with parmesan sprinkled over, if desired.

# Poached apricots with rosewater

**Prep:**5 mins **Cook:**15 mins Plus cooling

**Serves 2**

# Ingredients

- 50g golden caster sugar
- 400g ripe apricot , halved and stoned
- few drops rosewater
- Greek yogurt , to serve
- handful pistachios , roughly chopped, to serve

**Method**

**STEP 1**

Put the sugar into a medium pan with 150ml water. Heat gently until the sugar dissolves, then add the apricots and simmer for 15 mins until soft. Take off the heat, splash in the rosewater and leave to cool. Spoon into glasses to serve, topped with a few dollops of the yogurt and a scattering of nuts.

# Pan-fried rib-eye steak

**Prep:**5 mins **Cook:**10 mins

**Serves 2**

# Ingredients

- 2 rib-eye steaks, each about 200g and 2cm thick
- 1tbsp sunflower oil
- 1 tbsp/25g butter
- 1 garlic clove, left whole but bashed once
- thyme, optional

**Method**

**STEP 1**

Up to 8 hrs before cooking, pat the steaks dry with kitchen paper and season with salt and pepper. Heat the oil over a high flame in a heavy-based frying pan that will comfortably fit both steaks. When the oil is shimmering, turn the heat down to medium-high and add the butter. Once it's sizzling, carefully lay the steaks in the pan, tucking the garlic and herbs in at the sides.

**STEP 2**

Stand over the steaks with a pair of tongs, searing and turning them every 30 seconds to 1 min so they get a nice brown crust. As a rough guide, each steak will take 4 mins in total for rare, 5-6 mins in total for medium and 8-10 mins for well done. If you have a digital cooking thermometer, the temperatures you're looking for in middle of the steak are 50C for rare, 60C for medium and 70C for well done. Leave the steaks to rest for at least 5 mins. While the steaks are resting, you can make a classic red wine sauce to go with them.

# Moroccan-style chicken stew

**Prep:**10 mins **Cook:**20 mins

**Serves 4**

## Ingredients

- 1 tbsp olive oil
- 1 onion , chopped
- 1 garlic clove , crushed
- 1 tbsp ras-el-hanout or Moroccan spice mix
- 4 skinless chicken breasts , sliced
- 300ml reduced-salt chicken stock
- 400g can chickpeas , drained
- 12 dried apricots , sliced

- small bunch coriander , chopped

**Method**

**STEP 1**

Heat the oil in a large shallow pan, then cook the onion for 3 mins. Add the garlic and spices and cook for a further min. Tip in the chicken and cook for 3 mins, then pour in the chicken stock, chickpeas and apricots. Simmer for 5 mins or until the chicken is cooked through. Stir through the coriander and serve immediately with couscous and a green salad, if you like.

# Leek, tomato & barley risotto with pan-cooked cod

**Prep:**10 mins **Cook:**20 mins

**Serves 2**

# Ingredients

- 2 tsp rapeseed oil
- 1 large leek (315g), thinly sliced
- 2 garlic cloves , chopped
- 400g can barley (don't drain)
- 2 tsp vegetable bouillon
- 1 tsp finely chopped sage
- 1 tbsp thyme leaves , plus a few extra to serve
- 160g cherry tomatoes
- 50g finely grated parmesan
- 2 skin-on cod fillets or firm white fish fillets

**Method**

**STEP 1**

Heat 1 tsp oil in a non-stick pan and fry the leek and garlic for 5-10 mins, stirring frequently until softened, adding a splash of water to help it cook if you need to.

**STEP 2**

Tip in the barley with its liquid, then stir in the bouillon, sage and thyme. Simmer, stirring frequently for 3-4 mins. Add the tomatoes and cook about 4-5 mins more until they soften and start to split, adding a drop more water if necessary. Stir in the parmesan.

**STEP 3**

Meanwhile, heat the remaining oil in a non-stick pan and fry the cod, skin-side down, for 4-5 mins. Flip the fillets over to cook briefly on the other side. Spoon the risotto into two bowls. Serve the cod on top with a few thyme leaves, if you like.

# Green minestrone with tortellini

**Prep:**5 mins **Cook:**25 mins

**Serves 4**

## Ingredients

- 2 tbsp olive or rapeseed oil
- 1 onion , chopped
- 1 small leek , chopped
- 1 celery stick , chopped
- 3 garlic cloves , crushed
- 2 bay leaves
- 1l good-quality chicken or vegetable stock
- 100g shredded spring veg or cabbage
- 50g frozen peas
- 1 lemon , zested
- 250g tortellini

**Method**

**STEP 1**

Heat the olive or rapeseed oil in a large pan. Add the onion, leek and celery stick. Cook for 8-10 mins until softened, then stir in the garlic and bay leaves. Pour in the chicken or vegetable stock, then cover and simmer for 10 mins. Add the spring veg or cabbage, peas, lemon zest and tortellini (spinach tortellini works well). Cover and cook for another 3 mins, season well and ladle into bowls.

# Lighter moussaka with crunchy feta & oregano

**Prep:**10 mins **Cook:**50 mins

**Serves 4**

# Ingredients

- 300g extra-lean lamb mince
- 1 tsp olive oil
- 2 courgettes , finely chopped
- 1 large aubergine , finely chopped
- 140g red lentil
- 2 tsp dried oregano
- 680g jar passata with garlic & herbs
- 1 low-sodium lamb or beef stock cube
- 200g low-fat Greek yogurt
- 75g light feta cheese
- 2 tbsp breadcrumb
- salad and flatbreads , to serve (optional)

**Method**

**STEP 1**

Heat a dry non-stick pan and add the lamb, breaking it up with a fork. Cook until brown, then tip the meat into a bowl. Heat the oil in the pan and fry the courgettes and aubergines until golden, about 6-8 mins.

**STEP 2**

Return the meat to the pan and add the lentils, half the oregano and the passata. Crumble in the stock cube. Fill the passata jar to about half full with water (about 340ml), swirl and add to the pan. Simmer for 25-30 mins until the lentils are tender, adding more water if you need to. Season to taste.

**STEP 3**

Heat the grill to high. Mash together the rest of the oregano with the yogurt, feta and some seasoning. Pour the lamb mixture into 1 large or 4 individual ovenproof dishes, spoon over the topping, scatter on the crumbs, then grill for 3-4 mins until bubbling. Serve with salad and flatbreads, if you like.

# Easy vegan pho

**Prep:**10 mins **Cook:**20 mins

**Serves 2**

## Ingredients

- 100g rice noodles
- 1 tsp Marmite
- 1 tsp vegetable oil
- 50g chestnut mushrooms , sliced
- 1 leek , sliced
- 2 tbsp soy sauce

**To serve**

- 1 red chilli , sliced (deseeded if you don't like it too hot)
- ½ bunch mint , leaves picked and stalk discarded
- handful salted peanuts
- sriracha , to serve

**Method**

**STEP 1**

Tip the noodles into a bowl and cover with boiling water. Leave to stand for 10 mins, then drain, rinse in cold water and set aside.

**STEP 2**

In a jug, mix the Marmite with 500ml boiling water. Set aside while you cook the vegetables.

**STEP 3**

Heat the oil in a saucepan, then add the mushrooms and leek. Cook for 10-15 mins until softened and beginning to colour, then add the soy sauce and Marmite and water mixture and stir. Bring to the boil for 5 mins.

## STEP 4

Divide the noodles between two deep bowls, then ladle over the hot broth. Top with the chilli slices, mint leaves and peanuts, and serve with some sriracha on the side.

# Vegetable fried rice

**Prep:**2 mins **Cook:**8 mins

**Serves 2**

## Ingredients

- 1 bag stir-fry vegetables
- a pouch of cooked rice
- 2 eggs
- 2 tbsp teriyaki sauce

**Method**

## STEP 1

In a wok, stir-fry the vegetables for 1-2 mins until softening, then add the rice and warm through. Crack in the eggs and stir through with the teriyaki sauce.

# Tomato & rice soup

**Prep:**10 mins **Cook:**35 mins

**Serves 4**

## Ingredients

- 2 tsp olive oil
- 1 onion , finely chopped
- 1 carrot , finely chopped
- 1 celery stick, finely chopped
- 1 tbsp golden caster sugar
- 2 tbsp vinegar (white, red or balsamic)
- 1 tbsp tomato purée

- 400g can chopped tomato or passata
- 1l vegetable stock made with 2 cubes
- 140g rice (long-grain, basmati, wild, brown or a mixture)
- ¼ small pack parsley , leaves only, chopped, and a few drops of pesto, to serve (optional)

**Method**

**STEP 1**

Heat the oil in a large saucepan and add the onion, carrot and celery, then cook gently until softened. Add the sugar and vinegar, cook for 1 min, then stir through the tomato purée. Add the chopped tomatoes or passata, the vegetable stock, and any brown rice, if using, then cover and simmer for 10 mins. If you are using wild rice, add this and simmer for 10 mins more. Finally, add any white rice you're using, and simmer for a final 10 mins until the rice is tender.

**STEP 2**

Just before serving, sprinkle over some chopped parsley and season to taste. Divide into bowls and add a swirl of pesto to each, if you like.

# Seared beef salad with capers & mint

**Prep:** 10 mins **Cook:** 12 mins

**Serves 2**

# Ingredients

- 150g new potatoes , thickly sliced
- 160g fine green beans , trimmed and halved
- 160g frozen peas
- rapeseed oil , for brushing
- 200g lean fillet steak , trimmed of any fat
- 160g romaine lettuce , roughly torn into pieces

**For the dressing**

- 1 tbsp extra virgin olive oil
- 2 tsp cider vinegar
- ½ tsp English mustard powder
- 2 tbsp chopped mint

- 3 tbsp chopped basil
- 1 garlic clove , finely grated
- 1 tbsp capers

**Method**

## STEP 1

Cook the potatoes in a pan of simmering water for 5 mins. Add the beans and cook 5 mins more, then tip in the peas and cook for 2 mins until all the vegetables are just tender. Drain.

## STEP 2

Meanwhile, measure all the dressing ingredients in a large bowl and season with black pepper. Stir and crush the herbs and capers with the back of a spoon to intensify their flavours.

## STEP 3

Brush a little oil over the steak and grind over some black pepper. Heat a non-stick frying pan over a high heat and cook the steak for 4 mins on one side and 2-3 mins on the other, depending on the thickness and how rare you like it. Transfer to a plate to rest while you carry on with the rest of the salad.

## STEP 4

Mix the warm vegetables into the dressing until well coated, then add the lettuce and toss again. Pile onto plates. Slice the steak and turn in any dressing left in the bowl, add to the salad and serve while still warm.

# Minty griddled chicken & peach salad

**Prep:** 10 mins **Cook:** 15 mins

**Serves 2**

# Ingredients

- 1 lime , zested and juiced
- 1 tbsp rapeseed oil
- 2 tbsp mint , finely chopped, plus a few leaves to serve
- 1 garlic clove , finely grated
- 2 skinless chicken breast fillets (300g)

- 160g fine beans , trimmed and halved
- 2 peaches (200g), each cut into 8 thick wedges
- 1 red onion , cut into wedges
- 1 large Little Gem lettuce (165g), roughly shredded
- ½ x 60g pack rocket
- 1 small avocado , stoned and sliced
- 240g cooked new potatoes

**Method**

**STEP 1**

Mix the lime zest and juice, oil and mint, then put half in a bowl with the garlic. Thickly slice the chicken at a slight angle, add to the garlic mixture and toss together with plenty of black pepper.

**STEP 2**

Cook the beans in a pan of water for 3-4 mins until just tender. Meanwhile, griddle the chicken and onion for a few mins each side until cooked and tender. Transfer to a plate, then quickly griddle the peaches. If you don't have a griddle pan, use a non-stick frying pan with a drop of oil.

**STEP 3**

Toss the warm beans and onion in the remaining mint mixture, and pile onto a platter or into individual shallow bowls with the lettuce and rocket. Top with the avocado, peaches and chicken and scatter over the mint. Serve with the potatoes while still warm.

# Artichoke, red onion & rosemary risotto

**Prep:**15 mins **Cook:**35 mins

**Serves 4**

# Ingredients

- 1 tbsp olive oil
- 2 red onions , sliced into thin wedges
- 2 red peppers , cut into chunks
- 2 tbsp rosemary needles

- 140g arborio risotto rice
- 150ml white wine
- 850ml low-salt vegetable stock
- 400g tin artichoke heart in water, drained and halved
- 2 tbsp grated parmesan or vegetarian alternative
- 2 tbsp toasted pine nuts

**Method**

## STEP 1

Heat the oil in a large frying pan or wok. Cook the onions gently for 6-7 mins until softened and browning. Add the peppers and rosemary and cook for a further 5 mins. Add rice and stir well.

## STEP 2

Pour in the wine and of the stock. Bring to the boil then reduce the heat and simmer gently, stirring occasionally until almost all the liquid is absorbed.

## STEP 3

Stir in another of the stock and simmer again, until it's all absorbed. Add the final with the artichokes and simmer again until rice is tender.

## STEP 4

Season and stir in the Parmesan and ½ the pine nuts. Scatter over the remainder and serve.

# Easy tomato pizzas

**Prep:**10 mins **Cook:**12 mins

**Makes 8 small pizzas**

# Ingredients

**For the dough**

- 450g strong white bread flour , plus more to dust
- 7g sachet fast-action yeast
- 2 tbsp extra-virgin olive oil , plus extra to serve
- 350ml warm water

**For the topping**

- about 5 tbsp roast tomato sauce (see tip below), or stir together 100ml passata and a crushed garlic clove
- 8 tomatoes (green, orange, red, yellow - all different shapes and sizes)
- your choice of toppings: goat's cheese (with rind), grated Parmesan or Parmesan shavings, handful rocket, prosciutto

**Method**

**STEP 1**

For the dough, put the flour, yeast and 2 tsp salt into a large bowl and mix. Make a well. Mix the oil and water in a jug, then tip into the bowl. Use a wooden spoon to work the liquid into the flour – it will seem pretty wet. Set the bowl aside for 15 mins. Leaving the dough like this will save you from lengthy kneading later.

**STEP 2**

Turn the dough onto a well-floured surface, flour your hands, then knead it very gently for about 2 mins until it is fairly even, soft and bouncy. Return the dough to the bowl, cover with oiled cling film, then let it rise in a warm place (or in the fridge overnight) until doubled in size.

**STEP 3**

When ready to cook, heat oven to 240C/220C fan/gas 9 or as hot as it will go, then put a baking sheet in on a high shelf. Dust another sheet with flour. Split the dough into 8, then roll 3 balls thinly into rough circles. Lift onto the floured sheet. Smear over a thin layer of the sauce, scatter over a few slices of tomato, season, then add sliced goat's or grated Parmesan cheese if you want to. Slide the sheet on top of the heated sheet. Bake for 12 mins or until golden and crisp and the tomatoes are starting to caramelise around the edges. Top with any fresh toppings, then drizzle with more olive oil to serve.

# Indian winter soup

**Prep:** 15 mins **Cook:** 30 mins

**Serves 4 - 6**

## Ingredients

- 100g pearl barley

- 2 tbsp vegetable oil
- ½ tsp brown mustard seeds
- 1 tsp cumin seeds
- 2 green chillies, deseeded and finely chopped
- 1 bay leaf
- 2 cloves
- 1 small cinnamon stick
- ½ tsp ground turmeric
- 1 large onion, chopped
- 2 garlic cloves, finely chopped
- 1 parsnip, cut into chunks
- 200g butternut squash, cut into chunks
- 200g sweet potato, cut into chunks
- 1 tsp paprika
- 1 tsp ground coriander
- 225g red lentils
- 2 tomatoes, chopped
- small bunch coriander, chopped
- 1 tsp grated ginger
- 1 tsp lemon juice

## Method

### STEP 1

Rinse the pearl barley and cook following pack instructions. When it is tender, drain and set aside. Meanwhile, heat the oil in a deep, heavy-bottomed pan. Fry the mustard seeds, cumin seeds, chillies, bay leaf, cloves, cinnamon and turmeric until fragrant and the seeds start to crackle. Tip in the onion and garlic, then cook for 5-8 mins until soft. Stir in the parsnip, butternut and sweet potato and mix thoroughly, making sure the vegetables are fully coated with the oil and spices. Sprinkle in the paprika, ground coriander and seasoning, and stir again.

### STEP 2

Add the lentils, pearl barley, tomatoes and 1.7 litres water. Bring to the boil then turn down and simmer until the vegetables are tender. When the lentils are almost cooked, stir in the chopped coriander, ginger and lemon juice.

# Quick banana ice cream

**Prep:**5 mins Plus freezing

**Serves 4**

## Ingredients

- 4 ripe bananas , cut into chunks
- 3-4 tbsp milk
- 2 tbsp toasted flaked almonds
- 2 tbsp ready-made toffee or chocolate sauce

**Method**

**STEP 1**

Pop the banana chunks on a flat tray and cover well. Freeze for at least 1 hr, or until frozen through. When ready to eat throw the banana into a food processor and whizz until smooth with enough of the milk to achieve a creamy texture. Scoop into 4 bowls or glasses, then top with the sauce and nuts.

# Curried turkey lettuce wraps

**Prep:**5 mins **Serves 2**

## Ingredients

- 100g natural yogurt
- 1 tsp curry powder
- 1 tsp tomato purée
- 2 tbsp raisins
- 100g cooked skinless turkey or chicken breast meat
- 8 Little Gem lettuces leaves
- 2 tsp sunflower seeds
- coriander leaves

**Method**

**STEP 1**

Mix the natural yogurt with the curry powder, tomato purée and raisins. Stir in the cooked turkey or chicken, then spoon onto the lettuce leaves. Scatter over the sunflower seeds and the coriander leaves.

# Fruity coconut creams

**Prep:**10 mins No cook

**Serves 4**

# Ingredients

- 1 x 50g/2oz sachet coconut cream
- 500g 0% Greek yogurt or tub quark
- 85g icing sugar , sieved
- few drops vanilla extract
- 2 kiwi fruit
- 400g can pineapple chunks

**Method**

**STEP 1**

Dissolve the coconut cream in 50ml boiling water, then leave to cool. Spoon the quark or yogurt into a mixing bowl, then stir in the icing sugar and vanilla. Combine with the coconut mix, then spoon into individual glasses. Chill until ready to serve.

**STEP 2**

Peel and chop the kiwi fruit into small pieces. Drain the pineapple, then chop the chunks into small pieces. Mix the fruit together, then spoon over the top of the coconut creams to serve.

# Mushroom & potato soup — not so good!

**Prep:**15 mins **Cook:**30 mins

**Serves 4**

# Ingredients

- 1 tbsp rapeseed oil

- 2 large onions , halved and thinly sliced
- 20g dried porcini mushrooms
- 3 tsp vegetable bouillon powder
- 300g chestnut mushrooms , chopped
- 3 garlic cloves , finely grated
- 300g potato , finely diced
- 2 tsp fresh thyme
- 4 carrots , finely diced
- 2 tbsp chopped parsley
- 8 tbsp bio yogurt
- 55g walnut pieces

**Method**

**STEP 1**

Heat the oil in a large pan. Tip in the onions and fry for 10 mins until golden. Meanwhile, pour 1.2 litres boiling water over the dried mushrooms and stir in the bouillon.

**STEP 2**

Add the fresh mushrooms and garlic to the pan with the potatoes, thyme and carrots, and continue to fry until the mushrooms soften and start to brown.

**STEP 3**

Pour in the dried mushrooms and stock, cover the pan and leave to simmer for 20 mins. Stir in the parsley and plenty of pepper. Ladle into bowls and serve each portion topped with 2 tbsp yogurt and a quarter of the walnuts. The rest can be chilled and reheated the next day.

# Sticky pork

Prep:5 mins **Cook:**30 mins

**Serves 4**

## Ingredients

- 500g piece pork fillet

**For the marinade**

- 4 tbsp soy sauce
- 1 tbsp clear honey
- finely grated zest and juice 1 orange
- large knob of root ginger , finely grated

**Method**

**STEP 1**

Tip all the marinade ingredients into a shallow dish and stir to combine. Coat the pork in the marinade and, if you have time, leave for 1 hr or even better overnight. Heat oven to 200C/fan 180C/gas 6.

**STEP 2**

Heat an ovenproof pan and take the pork out of the marinade. Brown on all sides, then baste over the rest of the marinade and roast the pork for 20 mins until cooked all the way through, basting with its juices every 5 mins or so. Serve the pork sliced with rice and your favourite steamed greens.

# Veggie okonomiyaki

**Prep:**15 mins **Cook:**10 mins

**Serves 2**

# Ingredients

- 3 large eggs
- 50g plain flour
- 50ml milk
- 4 spring onions , trimmed and sliced
- 1 pak choi , sliced
- 200g Savoy cabbage , shredded
- 1 red chilli , deseeded and finely chopped, plus extra to serve
- ½ tbsp low-salt soy sauce
- ½ tbsp rapeseed oil
- 1 heaped tbsp low-fat mayonnaise
- ½ lime , juiced
- sushi ginger , to serve (optional)

- wasabi , to serve (optional)

**Method**

**STEP 1**

Whisk together the eggs, flour and milk until smooth. Add half the spring onions, the pak choi, cabbage, chilli and soy sauce. Heat the oil in a small frying pan and pour in the batter. Cook, covered, over a medium heat for 7-8 mins. Flip the okonomiyaki into a second frying pan, then return it to the heat and cook for a further 7-8 mins until a skewer inserted into it comes out clean.

**STEP 2**

Mix the mayonnaise and lime juice together in a small bowl. Transfer the okonomiyaki to a plate, then drizzle over the lime mayo and top with the extra chilli and spring onion and the sushi ginger, if using. Serve with the wasabi on the side, if you like.

# Thai spiced turkey patties with noodle salad

**Prep:**15 mins **Cook:**10 mins

**Serves 4**

# Ingredients

- 400g turkey breast or fillet, roughly chopped
- 1 lemongrass stalk, finely chopped
- 2 garlic cloves , crushed
- zest and juice 1 lime
- 3 tbsp low-sodium soy sauce
- small bunch coriander , chopped
- 1 red chilli , deseeded and chopped
- 2 nests medium wheat noodles
- 300g pack mixed peppers stir-fry vegetables
- sweet chilli sauce , to serve (optional)

**Method**

**STEP 1**

Heat the grill to Medium. Put the turkey in a food processor and pulse until minced. Add the lemongrass, garlic and lime zest, and half the soy sauce, coriander and chilli, then pulse again until combined. Tip the mix into a bowl and add some black pepper. Shape into 8 patties, then transfer to a non-stick baking tray and grill for 3-4 mins each side, until cooked through.

## STEP 2

Meanwhile, soak the noodles following pack instructions, then drain and add the vegetables, the remaining soy sauce and the lime juice. Toss well, divide between plates and sprinkle with the remaining coriander and chilli. Serve with the turkey patties and some sweet chilli sauce for dipping, if you like.

# Prawn chow mein

**Prep:**5 mins **Cook:**20 mins

**Serves 4**

# Ingredients

- 3 nests medium egg noodles
- 140g broccoli , chopped into small florets
- 140g baby corn , halved
- 1 tbsp olive oil
- 1 red pepper , sliced
- 300g prawns

**For the sauce**

- 3 tbsp tomato ketchup
- 2 tbsp oyster sauce

**Method**

**STEP 1**

Cook the noodles, broccoli and corn in boiling water for 3-4 mins, or until tender. Drain and set aside. Heat the oil in a large frying pan or wok and fry the pepper for 3 mins, until starting to soften.

**STEP 2**

Tip in the noodles and vegetables along with the prawns and toss together. Add the sauce ingredients and heat everything through for 2-3 mins, until piping hot.

# Thai fried prawn & pineapple rice

**Prep:**10 mins **Cook:**15 mins

**Serves 4**

## Ingredients

- 2 tsp sunflower oil
- bunch spring onions , greens and whites separated, both sliced
- 1 green pepper , deseeded and chopped into small chunks
- 140g pineapple , chopped into bite-sized chunks
- 3 tbsp Thai green curry paste
- 4 tsp light soy sauce , plus extra to serve
- 300g cooked basmati rice (brown, white or a mix - about 140g uncooked rice)
- 2 large eggs , beaten
- 140g frozen peas
- 225g can bamboo shoots , drained
- 250g frozen prawns , cooked or raw
- 2-3 limes , 1 juiced, the rest cut into wedges to serve
- handful coriander leaves (optional)

**Method**

**STEP 1**

Heat the oil in a wok or non-stick frying pan and fry the spring onion whites for 2 mins until softened. Stir in the pepper for 1 min, followed by the pineapple for 1 min more, then stir in the green curry paste and soy sauce.

**STEP 2**

Add the rice, stir-frying until piping hot, then push the rice to one side of the pan and scramble the eggs on the other side. Stir the peas, bamboo shoots and prawns into the rice and eggs, then heat through for 2 mins until the prawns are hot and the peas tender. Finally, stir in the spring onion greens, lime juice and coriander, if using. Spoon into bowls and serve with extra lime wedges and soy sauce.

# Feta & clementine lunch bowl

**Prep:** 15 mins **Cook:** 15 mins

**Serves 2**

## Ingredients

- 1 red onion , halved and thinly sliced
- 1 lemon , zested and juiced
- 2 clementines , 1 zested, flesh sliced
- 2 garlic cloves , chopped
- 400g can green lentils , drained
- 1 tbsp balsamic vinegar
- 1 ½ tbsp rapeseed oil
- 1 red pepper , quartered and sliced
- 60g feta , crumbled
- small handful mint , chopped
- 4 walnut halves , chopped

**Method**

**STEP 1**

Mix the onion with the lemon juice, lemon and clementine zest and garlic.

**STEP 2**

Tip the lentils into two bowls or lunchboxes and drizzle over the balsamic and 1 tbsp oil. Heat the remaining oil in a large non-stick wok, add the pepper and stir-fry for 3 mins. Tip in half the onion and cook until tender. Pile on top of the lentils, then mix the clementines, remaining onions, feta, mint and walnut pieces.

# Mushroom brunch

**Prep:** 5 mins **Cook:** 12 mins - 15 mins

**Serves 4**

## Ingredients

- 250g mushrooms
- 1 garlic clove
- 1 tbsp olive oil
- 160g bag kale
- 4 eggs

**Method**

**STEP 1**

Slice the mushrooms and crush the garlic clove. Heat the olive oil in a large non-stick frying pan, then fry the garlic over a low heat for 1 min. Add the mushrooms and cook until soft. Then, add the kale. If the kale won't all fit in the pan, add half and stir until wilted, then add the rest. Once all the kale is wilted, season.

**STEP 2**

Now crack in the eggs and keep them cooking gently for 2-3 mins. Then, cover with the lid to for a further 2-3 mins or until the eggs are cooked to your liking. Serve with bread.

# Tuna, avocado & quinoa salad

**Prep:**5 mins **Cook:**20 mins

**Serves 2**

## Ingredients

- 100g quinoa
- 3 tbsp extra virgin olive oil
- juice 1 lemon
- ½ tbsp white wine vinegar
- 120g can tuna, drained
- 1 avocado, stoned, peeled and cut into chunks
- 200g cherry tomatoes on the vine, halved
- 50g feta, crumbled
- 50g baby spinach
- 2 tbsp mixed seeds, toasted

**Method**

## STEP 1

Rinse the quinoa under cold water. Tip into a saucepan, cover with water and bring to the boil. Reduce the heat and simmer for 15 mins until the grains have swollen but still have some bite. Drain, then transfer to a bowl to cool slightly.

## STEP 2

Meanwhile, in a jug, combine the oil, lemon juice and vinegar with some seasoning.

## STEP 3

Once the quinoa has cooled, mix with the dressing and all the remaining ingredients and season. Divide between plates or lunchboxes.

# Creamy linguine with ham, lemon & basil

**Prep:**10 mins **Cook:**15 mins

**Serves 6**

# Ingredients

- 400g linguine or spaghetti
- 90g pack prosciutto
- 1 tbsp olive oil
- juice 1 lemon
- 2 egg yolks
- 3 tbsp crème fraîche
- large handful basil leaves
- large handful grated parmesan , plus extra to serve, if you like

**Method**

**STEP 1**

Cook the linguine. Meanwhile, tear the ham into small pieces and fry in the olive oil until golden and crisp.

**STEP 2**

Drain the pasta, reserving a little of the cooking water, then return to the pan. Tip in the cooked ham. Mix together the lemon juice, egg yolks and crème fraîche, then add this to the pan along with the basil and Parmesan. Mix in with tongs, adding a little of the cooking water, if needed, to make a creamy sauce that coats the pasta. Serve with extra Parmesan grated over the top, if you like.

# Steamed bass with pak choi

**Prep:**10 mins **Cook:**5 mins

**Serves 2**

## Ingredients

- small piece of ginger , peeled and sliced
- 2 garlic cloves , finely sliced
- 3 spring onions , finely sliced
- 2 tbsp soy sauce
- 1 tbsp sesame oil
- splash of sherry (optional)
- 2 x fillets sea bass
- 2 heads pak choi , quartered

**Method**

**STEP 1**

In a small bowl, mix all of the ingredients, except the fish and the pak choi, together to make a soy mix. Line one tier of a two-tiered bamboo steamer loosely with foil. Lay the fish, skin side up, on the foil and spoon over the soy mix. Place the fish over simmering water and throw the pak choi into the second tier and cover it with a lid. Alternatively, add the pak choi to the fish layer after 2 mins of cooking – the closer the tier is to the steam, the hotter it is.

**STEP 2**

Leave everything to steam for 6-8 mins until the pak choi has wilted and the fish is cooked. Divide the greens between two plates, then carefully lift out the fish. Lift the foil up and drizzle the tasty juices back over the fish.

# Sausage & butternut squash shells

**Prep:**15 mins **Cook:**35 mins

**Serves 4**

# Ingredients

- 1 medium butternut squash , peeled and cut into medium chunks
- 1 ½ tbsp olive oil
- 2 garlic cloves , crushed
- 1 fennel bulb , thinly sliced (keep the green fronds to serve)
- 4 spring onions , thinly sliced
- 2 tsp chilli flakes
- 1 tsp fennel seeds
- 300g large pasta shells
- 3 pork sausages

**Method**

**STEP 1**

Put the squash in a microwaveable bowl with a splash of water. Cover with cling film and cook on high for 10 mins until soft. Tip into a blender.

**STEP 2**

Meanwhile, put a frying pan over a medium heat and pour in 1 tbsp olive oil. Add the garlic, sliced fennel, spring onions, half the chilli flakes, half the fennel seeds and a splash of water. Cook, stirring occasionally, for 5 mins until softened. Scrape into the blender with squash. Blitz to a smooth sauce, adding enough water to get to a creamy consistency. Season to taste.

**STEP 3**

Bring a pan of water to the boil and cook the pasta for 1 min less than the pack instructions. Put the frying pan back on the heat (don't bother washing it first – it's all flavour). Pour in the remaining oil, squeeze the sausagemeat from the skins into the pan and add the remaining chilli and remaining fennel seeds. Fry until browned and crisp, breaking down the sausagemeat with a spoon.

**STEP 4**

Drain the pasta and return to its pan on the heat. Pour in the butternut sauce and give everything a good mix to warm the sauce through. Divide between bowls and top with the crispy sausage mix and fennel fronds.

# Rhubarb & strawberry meringue pots

**Prep:**15 mins **Cook:**1 hr

**Serves 4**

## Ingredients

- 450g rhubarb, cut into 4cm/1½in chunks
- 100g golden caster sugar
- grated zest of 1 orange
- 1 tbsp strawberry conserve
- 2 eggs, separated

**Method**

**STEP 1**

Preheat the oven to 180C/ Gas 4/fan oven 160C. Put the rhubarb in an ovenproof dish, sprinkle over 50g/2oz of the sugar and the orange zest and stir together. Cover and bake in the oven for 35-40 minutes until tender. (Alternatively, you can cook the rhubarb with the sugar and zest in the microwave for 10 minutes on full power, stirring halfway through the cooking time, until just tender.)

**STEP 2**

Remove the rhubarb from the oven and allow to cool slightly. Stir in the conserve then the egg yolks. Divide the rhubarb mixture between four 175ml/6fl oz ramekins. Put on a baking sheet and cook in the oven for 10 minutes until lightly thickened.

**STEP 3**

While the rhubarb is cooking, whisk the egg whites until stiff. Sprinkle over half of the remaining sugar and whisk again. Gently fold in the rest of the sugar. Pile the meringue on top of the rhubarb to cover it completely and swirl the top. Return to the oven for 10 minutes until the meringue is puffy and golden. Serve immediately.

# Miso mushroom & tofu noodle soup

**Prep:** 10 mins **Cook:** 15 mins

**Serves 1**

## Ingredients

- 1 tbsp rapeseed oil
- 70g mixed mushrooms , sliced
- 50g smoked tofu , cut into small cubes
- ½ tbsp brown rice miso paste
- 50g dried buckwheat or egg noodles
- 2 spring onions , shredded

**Method**

**STEP 1**

Heat half the oil in a frying pan over a medium heat. Add the mushrooms and fry for 5-6 mins, or until golden. Transfer to a bowl using a slotted spoon and set aside. Add the remaining oil to the pan and fry the tofu for 3-4 mins, or until evenly golden.

**STEP 2**

Mix the miso paste with 325ml boiling water in a jug. Cook the noodles following pack instructions, then drain and transfer to a bowl. Top with the mushrooms and tofu, then pour over the miso broth. Scatter over the spring onions just before serving.

# Mexican egg roll

**Prep:** 5 mins **Cook:** 10 mins

**Serves 2**

## Ingredients

- 1 large egg
- a little rapeseed oil for frying
- 2 tbsp tomato salsa
- about 1 tbsp fresh coriander

**Method**

**STEP 1**

Beat the egg with 1 tbsp water. Heat the oil in a medium non-stick pan. Add the egg and swirl round the base of the pan, as though you are making a pancake, and cook until set. There is no need to turn it.

**STEP 2**

Carefully tip the pancake onto a board, spread with the salsa, sprinkle with the coriander, then roll it up. It can be eaten warm or cold – you can keep it for 2 days in the fridge.

# Puy lentils with spinach & sour cherries

**Prep:**5 mins **Cook:**20 mins

**Serves 4**

# Ingredients

- 2 tsp olive oil
- 4 shallots , finely chopped
- 250g pouch ready-to-eat puy lentils
- 300ml reduced-salt vegetable or chicken stock
- 140g dried sour cherries
- 400g spinach
- small pack parsley , leaves picked and chopped

**Method**

**STEP 1**

Heat the oil in a medium saucepan. Add the shallots and cook on a medium heat for 10 mins until softened. Add the Puy lentils, stock and sour cherries, and simmer for 10 mins. Remove from the heat and stir through the spinach and parsley.

# Tuna sweet potato jackets

**Prep:**10 mins **Cook:**20 mins

**Serves 4**

# Ingredients

- 4 small sweet potatoes (about 200g each)
- 185g can tuna in spring water, drained
- ½ red onion , finely sliced
- 1 small red chilli , deseeded and chopped
- juice 1 lime
- 6 tbsp Greek yogurt
- handful coriander leaves

**Method**

## STEP 1

Scrub the sweet potatoes and prick all over with a fork. Place on a microwaveable plate and cook on High for 18-20 mins, or until tender. Split in half and place each one, cut-side up, on a serving plate.

## STEP 2

Flake the drained tuna with a fork and divide between the sweet potatoes. Top with the red onion and chilli, then squeeze over the lime juice. Top with a dollop of yogurt and scatter over the coriander, to serve.

# New potato & tamarind salad

**Prep:**15 mins **Cook:**25 mins

**Serves 6**

# Ingredients

- 1 ½ tbsp tamarind pulp or paste
- 50g golden muscovado sugar
- 1 tbsp ground cumin
- thumb-sized piece ginger , chopped
- 1.2kg new potato
- 3 tbsp natural low-fat yogurt

- 4 tbsp chopped coriander

**Method**

**STEP 1**

To make the dressing, put the tamarind pulp in a small pan, pour over 75ml boiling water and add the sugar, cumin and ginger. Simmer, without a lid, until the dressing thickens and becomes syrupy, about 10-15 mins. It should have a pleasant tang – add extra sugar if needed.

**STEP 2**

While the tamarind is cooking, bring a large pan of salted water to the boil and add the potatoes. Return to the boil and cook for 15 mins until tender. Drain, then cool slightly before halving them. Transfer to a big mixing bowl and spoon over the dressing, gently stirring to make sure the potatoes are well coated. Drizzle over the yogurt, scatter over the coriander, and serve warm or at room temperature.

# Sesame salmon, purple sprouting broccoli & sweet potato mash

**Prep:**10 mins **Cook:**15 mins

**Serves 2**

## Ingredients

- 1 ½ tbsp sesame oil
- 1 tbsp low-salt soy sauce
- thumb-sized piece ginger, grated
- 1 garlic clove, crushed
- 1 tsp honey
- 2 sweet potatoes, scrubbed and cut into wedges
- 1 lime, cut into wedges
- 2 boneless skinless salmon fillets
- 250g purple sprouting broccoli
- 1 tbsp sesame seeds
- 1 red chilli, thinly sliced (deseeded if you don't like it too hot)

**Method**

## STEP 1

Heat oven to 200C/180 fan/ gas 6 and line a baking tray with parchment. Mix together 1/2 tbsp sesame oil, the soy, ginger, garlic and honey. Put the sweet potato wedges, skin and all, into a glass bowl with the lime wedges. Cover with cling film and microwave on high for 12-14 mins until completely soft.

## STEP 2

Meanwhile, spread the broccoli and salmon out on the baking tray. Spoon over the marinade and season. Roast in the oven for 10-12 mins, then sprinkle over the sesame seeds.

## STEP 3

Remove the lime wedges and roughly mash the sweet potato using a fork. Mix in the remaining sesame oil, the chilli and some seasoning. Divide between plates, along with the salmon and broccoli.

# Creamy smoked salmon, leek & potato soup

**Prep:**15 mins **Cook:**25 mins

**Serves 8**

# Ingredients

- large knob of butter
- 2 large leeks , halved and finely sliced
- 1 bay leaf
- 1kg floury potatoes , diced
- 1l chicken or vegetable stock
- 100ml double cream
- 200g smoked salmon , cut into strips
- small bunch chives , snipped

**Method**

## STEP 1

Heat the butter in a large saucepan and add the leeks and bay leaf. Cook over a low heat for 8-10 mins or until the leek is really soft, then stir through the potatoes until coated in the butter.

Pour over the stock and cream and bring to the simmer, then gently bubble for 10-15 mins until the potatoes are really tender. If freezing at this stage, slightly under-cook the potatoes, then defrost and bring back to a simmer to finish cooking them and continue the recipe.

## STEP 2

Add two-thirds of the smoked salmon, stir through and season. Serve the soup in deep bowls with the remaining smoked salmon and snipped chives on the top.

# Open leek & sweet potato pie

**Prep:**20 mins **Cook:**40 mins

**Serves 6**

## Ingredients

- 3 tbsp olive oil , plus extra for brushing
- 2 large leeks , washed and sliced
- 2 sweet potatoes , peeled and roughly chopped into 2cm cubes
- 1 tsp coriander seeds
- 1 tsp chilli flakes
- 2 fat garlic cloves , crushed
- 150g ricotta
- 2 large eggs
- 1 lemon , zested
- 100g robust leafy greens such as cavalo nero or kale, finely shredded, tough core removed
- 1 small pack dill , chopped
- 1 pack filo pastry (around 12 sheets)
- 80g goat's cheese
- 1 tsp nigella seeds (optional)
- peppery salad , to serve

**Method**

**STEP 1**

Heat the oil in a large ovenproof frying pan. Add the leeks and a pinch of salt, then cook over a medium heat for a couple of mins until beginning to wilt. Tip in the sweet potato, cover the pan then cook, stirring occasionally, for 15 mins until the potato is mostly softened. Stir in the coriander seeds, chilli flakes, garlic and season. Give everything a gentle stir – you want the potato to remain intact as much as possible – then remove the pan from the heat and set aside to cool slightly.

## STEP 2

In a large bowl, whisk together the ricotta, eggs and lemon zest with some seasoning. Stir in the greens and dill, then scrape in the sweet potato filling, (set aside the frying pan afterwards) and fold everything together. Heat oven to 220C/200C fan/gas 7.

## STEP 3

Lay your first sheet of filo in the frying pan you used for the sweet potato (no need to wash it first). Brush the top with a little oil, then continue to layer the filo, setting each sheet at a different angle and oiling in between the layers until all edges of the pan are covered. Spoon the filling on top of the pastry, dot over the goat's cheese, then crumple the pastry in over the filling, leaving the centre of the pie exposed. Brush the top with a little more oil and scatter over the nigella seeds, if using.

## STEP 4

Turn the hob back on and cook the pie over a medium-low heat for 3 mins to ensure the base is crisp, then transfer to the oven and bake for 12-15 mins until the pastry is crisp and golden. Let the pie cool in the pan for 10 mins before slicing.

# Apple & sultana porridge

**Prep:**10 mins **Cook:**5 mins

**Serves 4**

# Ingredients

- 100g porridge oat
- 500ml skimmed milk
- 4 apples , cored and diced
- 100g sultana
- 1 tbsp brown sugar , to serve

**Method**

**STEP 1**

Put the oats and milk in a small pan and cook, stirring, for 3 mins until almost creamy. Stir in the apples and sultanas, then cook for 2 mins more or until the porridge is thick and creamy and the apples just tender. Ladle into bowls, sprinkle with sugar and eat immediately.

# Chipotle chicken tacos with pineapple salsa

**Prep:**10 mins **Cook:**10 mins

**Serves 4**

## Ingredients

- 500g skinless boneless chicken thighs
- 1 tbsp vegetable oil
- 1 medium onion , chopped
- 2 tsp sweet smoked paprika
- 2 tsp ground cumin
- 2 tbsp cider vinegar
- 1 tbsp chipotle paste
- 200ml passata
- 2 tbsp soft brown sugar
- ½ small pineapple , cored, peeled and chopped
- ½ small pack coriander , chopped
- corn or flour tortillas
- hot sauce (I like Tabasco Chipotle), to serve

**Method**

**STEP 1**

In a food processor, roughly blitz the chicken thighs into chunky mince. Alternatively, chop into bite-sized pieces.

**STEP 2**

Heat the oil in a large saucepan. Add half the onion and the chicken mince. Season well and cook for about 5 mins on a high heat to brown, breaking up the meat with a spoon. Add the spices, vinegar, chipotle paste, passata and sugar. Cook for another 5 mins, then remove from the heat.

**STEP 3**

In a small bowl, mix the remaining onion, the pineapple and coriander. Serve the chicken and the pineapple salsa with warm tortillas and hot sauce.

# Peach crumble

**Prep:**10 mins **Cook:**35 mins

**Serves 6**

## Ingredients

- 3 x 410g cans peach slices in juice
- zest 1 lemon , plus juice ½
- 1 tbsp agave syrup
- 140g plain flour
- 50g porridge oat
- 25g cold butter , grated

**Method**

**STEP 1**

Heat oven to 200C/180C fan/gas 6. Drain the peaches, but reserve the juice. Tip the peaches into a deep baking dish, roughly 20 x 30cm. Scatter over the lemon zest and juice and 1 tbsp of the agave, then toss everything together.

**STEP 2**

In a bowl, combine the flour, oats, butter, remaining agave and 4 tbsp of the reserved peach juice. Mix together, first with a spoon, then with your fingers, until you have a rough crumbly mixture. Scatter over the peaches, then bake for 35 mins until golden and crunchy on top.

# Coriander cod with carrot pilaf

**Prep:**8 mins **Cook:**15 mins

**Serves 4**

## Ingredients

- 2 tbsp olive oil
- 4 skinless cod fillets, about 175g/6oz each
- 2 tbsp chopped coriander
- zest and juice 1 lemon
- 1 onion , chopped
- 2 tsp cumin seeds
- 2 large carrots , grated
- 200g basmati rice
- 600ml vegetable stock

### Method

### STEP 1

Heat the grill pan to high, then line with double thickness foil and curl up the edges to catch the juices. Brush lightly with oil and put the cod on top. Sprinkle over the coriander, lemon zest and juice and drizzle with a little more of the oil. Season with salt and pepper, then grill for 10-12 mins until the fish flakes easily.

### STEP 2

Meanwhile, heat the remaining oil in a pan. Add the onion and cumin and fry for a few mins. Add the carrots and stir well, then stir in the rice until glistening. Add the stock and bring to the boil. Cover and cook gently for about 10 mins until the rice is tender and the stock absorbed. Spoon the rice onto 4 warm plates, top with cod and pour over the pan juices.

# Ginger & lime chicken with sweet potato mash

Prep:15 mins Cook:20 mins Plus 10 mins marinating

Serves 2

## Ingredients

- zest and juice 1 lime
- 1 tbsp maple syrup or clear honey
- thumb-size piece fresh root ginger , cut into matchsticks, plus 1 tsp grated root ginger
- 2 skinless, boneless chicken breasts

- 450g/1lb sweet potatoes , roughly chopped
- 1 tbsp olive oil

**Method**

### STEP 1

Mix half the lime zest and all the juice with the maple syrup and grated ginger. Slash each chicken breast 3-4 times with a sharp knife, then coat well with the marinade. Set aside for 10 mins. Heat the grill and line the grill tray with foil.

### STEP 2

Cook the sweet potatoes in salted boiling water for 10-12 mins until tender. Drain and mash well, adding the rest of the lime zest, plus some seasoning. Meanwhile, grill the chicken breasts for 10-15 mins, until cooked through and slightly caramelised.

### STEP 3

Heat the oil in a small frying pan. When it's really hot, add the ginger matchsticks and fry for 1 min until the ginger is crisp. Lift out the matchsticks with a slotted spoon, then stir the mash into the gingerinfused oil. Divide the mash between 2 plates, top each with a chicken breast, scatter with the crisp ginger and serve with some sugar snap peas.

# Easy lentil curry

**Prep:**5 mins **Cook:**45 mins

**Serves 4**

# Ingredients

- 2 tbsp sunflower oil
- 2 medium onions, cut into rough wedges
- 4 tbsp curry paste
- 850ml vegetable stock
- 750g stewpack frozen vegetables
- 100g red lentil
- 200g basmati rice
- turmeric
- handful of raisins and roughly chopped parsley

- poppadums and mango chutney, to serve

**Method**

**STEP 1**

Heat the oil in a large pan. Add the onions and cook over a high heat for about 8 minutes or until they are golden brown. Stir in the curry paste and cook for a minute. Slowly pour in a little of the stock so it sizzles, scraping any bits from the bottom of the pan. Gradually pour in the rest of the stock.

**STEP 2**

Stir the frozen vegetables, cover and simmer for 5 minutes. Add the lentils and simmer for a further 15-20 minutes or until the vegetables and lentils are cooked.

**STEP 3**

While the curry is simmering, cook the rice according to the packet instructions, adding the turmeric to the cooking water. Drain well.

**STEP 4**

Season the curry with salt, toss in a handful of raisins and chopped parsley, then serve with the rice, poppadums and chutney.

# Curried aubergine & potato pie

**Prep:**10 mins **Cook:**1 hr - 1 hr and 10 mins

**Serves 4**

## Ingredients

- 1kg potato , peeled and cut into 3cm chunks
- 1 tbsp olive oil
- 1 large onion , chopped
- 2 large garlic cloves , crushed
- 2 medium aubergines , cut into 3cm chunks
- 1 tbsp medium curry powder
- 400g can chopped tomato
- 2 tbsp tomato purée

- 410g can green lentil , drained

**Method**

### STEP 1

Preheat the oven to fan 200C/conventional 220C/gas 7. Cook the potatoes in lightly salted simmering water for 15-20 minutes until just tender – don't let the water boil or the potatoes will break up.

### STEP 2

Meanwhile, heat the oil in a large frying pan and gently fry the onion and garlic until starting to go golden – about 4-5 minutes. Remove 2 tbsp of onion mixture and set aside.

### STEP 3

Add the aubergines to the pan. Cook gently, stirring now and then, for 6-8 minutes, until softened. Stir in the curry powder. Cook for 30 seconds then add the tomatoes, tomato purée and lentils. Cook for 1-2 minutes, then transfer to a 2 litre dish. Drain the potatoes, pile on top of the aubergine mixture and sprinkle over the reserved onion mixture. (At this stage it can be frozen for up to one month.)

### STEP 4

Bake for 30-35 minutes until nicely browned on top. Serve with broccoli or a salad.

# Spinach & barley risotto

**Prep:** 10 mins **Cook:** 15 mins

**Serves 2**

## Ingredients

- 2 tsp rapeseed oil
- 1 large leek (315g), thinly sliced
- 2 garlic cloves , chopped
- 2 x 400g can barley , undrained
- 1 tbsp vegetable bouillon powder

- 1 tsp finely chopped sage
- 1 tbsp thyme leaves
- 160g cherry tomatoes , halved
- 160g spinach
- 50g finely grated vegetarian Italian-style hard cheese

**Method**

**STEP 1**

Heat the oil in a non-stick pan and fry the leek and garlic for 5-10 mins, stirring frequently, until softened, adding a splash of water if it sticks.

**STEP 2**

Tip in the cans of barley and their liquid, then stir in the bouillon powder, sage and thyme. Simmer, stirring frequently, for 4-5 mins. Add the tomatoes and spinach and cook for 2-3 mins more until the spinach is wilted, adding a splash more water if needed. Stir in most of the cheese, then serve with the remaining cheese scattered over.

# Braised baby leeks

**Prep:**5 mins **Cook:**20 mins

**Serves 2**

## Ingredients

- 280g baby leeks
- knob of butter
- 500ml chicken stock
- handful thyme sprigs , plus extra leaves to serve

**Method**

**STEP 1**

Wash and trim the ends and roots of the baby leeks. Heat a knob of butter in a large frying pan, and add the leeks. Roll them around to coat them in the butter.

**STEP 2**

Add the chicken stock, bring to the boil, then turn down to a simmer and add the thyme. Cook for 20 mins or until tender. Serve with a sprinkling of thyme leaves.

# Turkey & avocado toast

**Prep:** 10 mins **Cook:** 5 mins

**Serves 2**

## Ingredients

- 1 avocado
- juice ½ lime
- 2-3 small slices ciabatta bread
- 100g turkey slices

**Method**

**STEP 1**

Halve and stone the avocado then scrape out the flesh into a bowl. Squeeze in the lime, season, then mash roughly with a fork. Toast the ciabatta, spread with mashed avocado, top with turkey and finish with ground black pepper.

# Herb & garlic baked cod with romesco sauce & spinach

**Prep:** 10 mins **Cook:** 20 mins

**Serves 2**

## Ingredients

- 2 x 140g skinless cod loin or pollock fillets
- 1 tbsp rapeseed oil, plus 2 tsp
- 1 tsp fresh thyme leaves
- 1 large garlic clove, finely grated
- ½ lemon, zested and juiced
- 1 large red pepper, sliced
- 2 leeks, well washed and thinly sliced

- 2 tbsp flaked almonds
- 1 tbsp tomato purée
- ¼ tsp vegetable bouillon powder
- 1 tsp apple cider vinegar
- 100g baby spinach, wilted in a pan or the microwave

**Method**

**STEP 1**

Heat oven to 220C/200C fan/ gas 7 and put the fish fillets in a shallow ovenproof dish so they fit quite snugly in a single layer. Mix 1 tbsp rapeseed oil with the thyme and garlic, spoon over the fish, then grate over the lemon zest. Bake for 10-12 mins until the fish is moist and flakes easily when tested.

**STEP 2**

Meanwhile, heat the remaining oil in a non-stick pan and fry the pepper and leeks for 5 mins until softened. Add the almonds and cook for 5 mins more. Tip in the tomato purée, 5 tbsp water, the bouillion powder and vinegar, and cook briefly to warm the mixture through.

**STEP 3**

Add the juice of up to half a lemon and blitz with a stick blender until it makes a thick, pesto-like sauce. Serve with the fish and the wilted spinach.

# Chicken with crispy Parma ham

**Prep:** 10 mins **Cook:** 20 mins

**Serves 4**

## Ingredients

- 450g new potato , halved if large
- 225g runner bean , trimmed and sliced
- 4 skinless chicken breasts
- 1 tbsp olive oil
- 4 slices Parma ham
- 1 garlic clove , crushed
- juice 1 lemon

**Method**

**STEP 1**

Cook the new potatoes in boiling salted water for 10-15 mins, until just tender, adding the green beans for the final 2 mins. Meanwhile, put each chicken breast between two sheets of cling film and bash them with a rolling pin until they're about 1cm thick. Season.

**STEP 2**

Heat a large frying pan and add the Parma ham. Cook for 2 mins, until crisp. Drain on kitchen paper. Add the oil to the pan and add two of the chicken breasts. Cook for 3 mins each side, transfer to a plate and keep warm. Cook the other two breasts in the same way.

**STEP 3**

Remove the pan from the heat and add the garlic and lemon juice. Toss in the drained beans and potatoes and crumble in the Parma ham. Divide the chicken and veg between four plates.

# Five-spice beef & sugar snap noodles

**Prep:** 10 mins **Cook:** 15 mins

**Serves 4**

# Ingredients

- 250g lean minced beef
- 3 nests medium egg noodles
- thumb-sized piece ginger , finely grated
- 3 garlic cloves , finely grated
- 1 heaped tsp five-spice powder
- ¼ tsp chilli powder
- 225g pack mangetout or sugar snap peas
- 400ml beef stock
- 3 tbsp light soy sauce , or more to taste
- sesame oil , to serve
- red chilli , deseeded and shredded to serve (optional)

**Method**

**STEP 1**

Heat a large non-stick frying pan or wok, then fry the beef for 10 mins until very well browned. Don't add any oil. Meanwhile, boil the noodles following pack instructions, then drain.

**STEP 2**

Add the ginger, garlic, five-spice, chilli powder and mangetout to the browned mince, then fry for a few mins more until fragrant and the pods are bright green. Splash in the stock, add the noodles, then season with the soy sauce. Pile into bowls (use tongs, it's easier), sprinkling with the sesame oil and red chilli if using.

# Lemony salmon & lettuce wraps

**Prep:** 10 mins no cook

**Serves 2**

## Ingredients

- 400g can cannellini beans , rinsed and drained
- 213g can wild red salmon , drained, skin and bones removed if you like
- ½ lemon , zested and juiced
- 1 spring onion , finely chopped
- 1 tbsp Greek yogurt
- 1 tbsp dill , chopped
- 8 large romaine lettuce leaves

**Method**

**STEP 1**

Mix together all the ingredients except the lettuce in a bowl.

**STEP 2**

Trim the chunky part of the stalk at the base of each lettuce leaf so they are easier to roll up, then place the leaves in pairs on top of each other, head to toe. Spoon on the salmon mixture, then roll up and keep in place with strips of baking parchment, which make the wraps easier to hold and eat. Pack into a container to keep the wraps from getting crushed and, if possible, chill to keep the lettuce crisp.

# Chicken & avocado sandwich topper

**Prep:**5 mins No cook

**Serves 1**

## Ingredients

- 2 tsp low-fat mayonnaise
- slices cooked chicken
- ½ small avocado , diced
- squeeze of lemon
- chopped red onion
- coriander leaves
- halved cherry tomatoes
- slice wholemeal seeded bread or rye, or wholegrain pitta, to serve

**Method**

**STEP 1**

Top bread or fill pitta with mayonnaise and chicken then add avocado, lemon, red onion, coriander and cherry tomatoes.

# Raspberry chia jam

**Prep:**5 mins **Cook:**15 mins Plus cooling

**Makes 1 jar (about 400g)**

## Ingredients

- 500g raspberries
- 1 tsp vanilla bean paste
- 3 tbsp honey
- 3 tbsp chia seeds

**Method**

**STEP 1**

Put the raspberries in a pan with the vanilla and honey, then cook over a low heat for 5 mins or until the berries have broken down.

## STEP 2

Stir through the chia and cook for 10 mins. Set aside to cool completely (it will thicken significantly as it cools). Spoon into a bowl or sterilised jar. Great on toast, swirled through porridge or in yogurt. Will keep in the fridge for up to one week.

# Thai-style fish broth with greens

**Prep:**10 mins **Cook:**15 mins

**Serves 2**

# Ingredients

- 100g brown rice noodle
- 500ml chicken or fish stock
- 1 tbsp Thai red curry paste
- 4 dried or fresh kaffir lime leaves
- 1 tbsp fish sauce
- 200g skinless sustainable white fish , such as pollock
- 100g raw king prawn
- 2 pak choi , leaves separated
- handful coriander leaves

**Method**

## STEP 1

Cook the noodles following pack instructions. Refresh in cold water and drain well.

## STEP 2

Put the stock in a large saucepan and stir in the curry paste, lime leaves, fish sauce and 250ml cold water. Bring to a simmer and cook for 5 mins.

## STEP 3

Cut the fish into roughly 3cm cubes and add to the pan. Return to a simmer, then cook for 2 mins uncovered.

**STEP 4**

Stir in the noodles, prawns and pak choi, and simmer for 2-3 mins or until the fish and prawns are just cooked. Serve in bowls scattered with coriander.

# Pepper & lemon spaghetti with basil & pine nuts

**Prep:**7 mins **Cook:**25 mins

**Serves 2**

# Ingredients

- 1 tbsp rapeseed oil
- 1 red pepper , deseeded and diced
- 150g wholemeal spaghetti
- 2 courgettes (250g), grated
- 2 garlic cloves , finely grated
- 1 lemon , zested and juiced
- 15g basil , finely chopped
- 25g pine nuts , toasted
- 2 tbsp finely grated parmesan or vegetarian alternative (optional)

**Method**

**STEP 1**

Heat the oil in a large non-stick frying pan. Add the pepper and cook for 5 mins. Meanwhile, cook the pasta for 10-12 mins until tender.

**STEP 2**

Add the courgette and garlic to the pepper and cook, stirring very frequently, for 10-15 mins until the courgette is really soft.

**STEP 3**

Stir in the lemon zest and juice, basil and spaghetti (reserve some pasta water) and toss together, adding a little of the pasta water until nicely coated. Add the pine nuts, then spoon into bowls and serve topped with the parmesan, if using.

# Pasta with tuna & tomato sauce

**Total time**35 mins Ready in 30-35 minutes

**Serves 4**

## Ingredients

- 2 tbsp olive oil
- 1 onion, chopped
- 2 garlic cloves, finely chopped
- 400g can chopped tomatoes with herbs
- ½ tsp chilli powder
- 1 tsp sugar
- 500g pkt pasta bows
- 100g can tuna, drained
- handful of basil leaves, optional

**Method**

**STEP 1**

Heat the oil in a pan, throw in the onion and cook for a couple of minutes. Stir in the garlic, tomatoes, chilli and sugar. Season with salt and pepper and bring to the boil. Give it a good stir, then reduce the heat and simmer for 5 minutes.

**STEP 2**

Meanwhile, bring a large pan of salted water to the boil. Add the pasta and cook according to packet instructions. Flake the tuna into the sauce and heat through. Drain the pasta, return to the pan and stir in the sauce and basil leaves if you have any. Serve with a generous grinding of pepper.

# Oaty fish & prawn gratins

**Prep:**12 mins **Cook:**28 mins

**Serves 2**

## Ingredients

- 340g bag baby spinach , roughly chopped
- 400g can chopped tomato with garlic and herbs
- 225g sustainable white fish fillets, chopped into large chunks
- small bunch basil , shredded
- 100g cooked and peeled prawn
- 2 tbsp finely grated parmesan
- 2 tbsp breadcrumb
- 2 tbsp oats
- 170g broccoli , boiled or steamed, to serve

**Method**

**STEP 1**

Put the spinach in a large colander and pour over boiling water. Once cool enough to handle, squeeze out any excess water, then season.

**STEP 2**

Tip the tomatoes into a frying pan with some seasoning and simmer for 5 mins to thicken. Add the fish and heat for 1-2 mins – it doesn't need to be fully cooked at this point. Stir in the basil.

**STEP 3**

Heat oven to 220C/200C fan/gas 7. Divide the spinach, fish, prawns and tomato sauce between 2 gratin dishes. Mix the Parmesan, breadcrumbs and oats together and sprinkle over the top. Bake for 20 mins until golden and bubbling. Serve with cooked broccoli.

# Skinny chicken Caesar salad

**Prep:**30 mins **Cook:**10 mins - 12 mins

**Serves 4**

# Ingredients

- 4 skinless chicken breasts
- 2 tsp olive oil
- juice 1 lemon
- 1 large Romaine or Cos lettuce , chopped into large pieces
- 1 punnet salad cress

- 4 hard-boiled eggs , peeled and quartered
- 25g parmesan , finely grated
- 50g anchovy fillets, half chopped, half left whole
- 170g pot fat-free Greek yogurt

**Method**

**STEP 1**

Put the chicken breasts in a large bowl with the olive oil and 1 tbsp lemon juice, then season. Heat the grill to high. Put the chicken breasts on a foil-lined tray and cook under the grill for 10-12 mins until golden and cooked through, turning once during cooking. Transfer to a plate or board and slice.

**STEP 2**

Arrange the lettuce, cress and eggs on a platter or serving plates and top with the cooked chicken. Mix together the Parmesan, chopped anchovies, yogurt and remaining lemon juice, season to taste and pour over the salad. Arrange the whole anchovy fillets on top of each salad.

# Chocolate chia pudding

**Prep:**5 mins No cook, plus 4 hours chilling

**Serves 4**

## Ingredients

- 60g chia seeds
- 400ml unsweetened almond milk or hazelnut milk
- 3 tbsp cacao powder
- 2 tbsp maple syrup
- ½ tsp vanilla extract
- cacao nibs , mixed
- frozen berries , to serve

**Method**

**STEP 1**

Put all the ingredients in a large bowl with a generous pinch of sea salt and whisk to combine. Cover with cling film then leave to thicken in the fridge for at least 4 hours, or overnight.

**STEP 2**

Spoon the pudding into four glasses, then top with the frozen berries and cacao nibs.

# Leek, mushroom & goat's cheese strudels

**Prep:**20 mins **Cook:**40 mins

**Serves 4**

# Ingredients

- 500g leeks , thinly sliced
- 150ml low-sodium vegetable stock
- 175g chestnut mushroom , sliced
- 4 large sheets filo pastry
- 1 tbsp olive oil
- 85g soft-rinded goat's cheese or vegetarian alternative
- 1 tsp poppy seeds

**Method**

**STEP 1**

Heat oven to 200C/180C fan/gas 6. Put the leeks and stock into a large pan, then cover and cook for 5-8 mins until starting to soften. Add the mushrooms, cover again and cook for 3 mins, then remove the lid and continue to cook until the juices have evaporated. Tip the veg onto a large plate to cool slightly.

**STEP 2**

For each strudel, lightly brush half of each filo sheet with some olive oil. Fold the un-brushed side over to make a smaller sheet, 2 layers thick. Brush the edges with a little more oil, then spoon a quarter of the veg along one edge. Crumble over a quarter of the cheese, fold over the pastry edges, then roll up to seal in the filling.

**STEP 3**

Put the strudels on a baking tray, brush with any remaining oil and scatter over the poppy seeds. Bake for 25 mins until crisp and golden brown.

# Cabbage with caraway

**Prep:** 10 mins **Cook:** 10 mins

**Serves 4**

## Ingredients

- 1 Savoy cabbage , cored and shredded
- 1 tbsp olive oil
- 1 onion , thinly sliced
- 2-3 tsp caraway seeds

**Method**

**STEP 1**

Cook the cabbage in boiling water for 3 mins until tender, then drain. Heat the oil in a frying pan. Add the onion and cook for 2-3 mins until starting to soften and turn golden. Sprinkle over the caraway seeds and cook for a further 2 mins until fragrant. Stir in the cabbage and heat through.

# Lime prawn cocktail pitta salad

**Prep:** 10 mins **Cook:** 15 mins

**Serves 2**

## Ingredients

- ½ wholemeal pitta
- ½ tbsp rapeseed oil
- 1 tsp Tabasco
- 1 tsp low-sugar, low-salt ketchup
- 1 tbsp low-fat mayonnaise
- 1 tbsp fat-free natural yogurt

- ½ lime , zested and juiced, plus wedges to serve
- 60g cooked king prawns
- 1 Little Gem lettuce , leaves separated
- ¼ small cucumber , peeled into ribbons
- 4 cherry tomatoes , halved

**Method**

**STEP 1**

Heat the oven to 200C/180C fan/gas 6. Slice the pitta into triangles, put on a baking sheet and drizzle over the oil. Bake for 10-15 mins until golden and crisp.

**STEP 2**

Mix together the Tabasco, ketchup, mayo, yogurt and lime zest and juice. Toss the prawns in the dressing.

**STEP 3**

Layer the lettuce, cucumber, tomatoes and dressed prawns in a lunchbox or jar. Season, top with the pitta chips and serve with lime wedges.

# Ham, mushroom & spinach frittata

**Prep:**4 mins **Cook:**9 mins

**Serves 2**

# Ingredients

- 1 tsp oil
- 80g chestnut mushrooms , sliced
- 50g ham , diced
- 80g bag spinach
- 4 medium eggs , beaten
- 1 tbsp grated cheddar

**Method**

**STEP 1**

Heat the grill to its highest setting. Heat the oil in an ovenproof frying pan over a medium-high heat. Tip in the mushrooms and fry for 2 mins until mostly softened. Stir in the ham and spinach, and cook for 1 min more until the spinach has wilted. Season well with black pepper and a pinch of salt.

## STEP 2

Reduce the heat and pour over the eggs. Cook undisturbed for 3 mins until the eggs are mostly set. Sprinkle over the cheese and put under the grill for 2 mins. Serve hot or cold.

# Crunchy detox salad

**Prep:** 15 mins - 20 mins **Cook:** 1 min

**Serves 4**

# Ingredients

- 250g broccoli , cut into small florets
- 100g ready-to-eat dried apricots , cut into strips
- 300g red cabbage , finely shredded
- 400g can chickpeas , rinsed and drained
- 50g sunflower seeds
- 1 small red onion , finely sliced
- 2cm piece ginger , grated
- juice 1 small orange
- 1 tbsp balsamic vinegar
- 2 tsp olive oil

**Method**

**STEP 1**

Blanch the broccoli in a pan of boiling water for 1 min. Drain and quickly cool under cold running water, then pat dry with kitchen paper. Put in a bowl with the apricots, broccoli, red cabbage, chickpeas and sunflower seeds.

**STEP 2**

Put the onion and ginger in a bowl with the orange juice, vinegar and oil. Mix well. Leave for 5 mins to soften the onion, then add to the salad and thoroughly toss everything together.

# Peach Melba smoothie

**Prep:** 5 mins No cook

**Serves 2**

## Ingredients

- 410g can peach halves
- 100g frozen raspberry , plus a few for garnish
- 100ml orange juice
- 150ml fresh custard , plus a spoonful for garnish

**Method**

**STEP 1**

Drain and rinse peaches and place in a blender with raspberries. Add orange juice and fresh custard and whizz together.

**STEP 2**

Pour over ice, garnish with another spoonful of custard and a few raspberries. Best served chilled.

# Ham hock & cabbage hash

**Prep:** 15 mins **Cook:** 35 mins

**Serves 5**

## Ingredients

- 1kg potato , unpeeled and cut into cubes
- 25g butter
- ½ Savoy cabbage , shredded
- 1 onion , thinly sliced
- 100ml low-sodium vegetable stock
- 175g ham hock, shredded
- baked beans and your favourite sauce, to serve

**Method**

**STEP 1**

Cook the potatoes in a large pan of salted water until tender, drain, then allow to steam dry for about 3 mins.

**STEP 2**

Meanwhile, melt half the butter in a large non-stick frying pan, then throw in the cabbage and onion and fry for 2 mins. Add the stock and cook for 5 mins more until the veg is starting to soften. Stir in the ham and potatoes and push down in the pan to flatten slightly. Cook for 8 mins until the base is golden and crisp.

**STEP 3**

Heat the grill. Dot the remaining butter on top of the hash, then flash under the grill until golden and crisp. Serve with baked beans and brown sauce or ketchup, if you like.

# Chicken & mushroom pancake topping

**Prep:** 5 mins **Cook:** 15 mins

**Serves 4**

## Ingredients

- a large knob of butter
- 250g chopped chestnut mushrooms
- 1 crushed garlic clove
- 2 tbsp flour
- 250ml milk
- 2 tsp Dijon mustard
- 2 tbsp mushroom ketchup
- 2 cooked chicken breasts
- a handful chopped parsley

**Method**

**STEP 1**

Melt the butter in a pan, add the mushrooms and cook until softened, about 8 mins. Add the garlic and cook for 1 min more, then stir in the flour, milk, mustard and ketchup. Stir for a few mins until you have a thick sauce, then season well.

## STEP 2

Shred the chicken and add to the sauce along with the parsley. Top four warm pancakes (see our easy pancakes recipe) with the chicken & mushroom mix and serve.

# Crisp chicken burgers with lemon mayo

**Prep:** 10 mins **Cook:** 10 mins

Serves 4

# Ingredients

- 4 chicken breasts
- 3 slices white bread , toasted
- 1 egg
- 1 tsp Dijon mustard
- zest 1 lemon , juice from ½
- 4 tbsp reduced-fat mayonnaise
- 4 ciabatta buns, warm or toasted

**Method**

## STEP 1

Heat grill to high. Put the chicken breasts between 2 pieces of cling film and bash with a rolling pin until they're about half their original thickness. Whizz the toast in a food processor to rough breadcrumbs, then tip out onto a plate.

## STEP 2

Beat the egg and mustard together in a bowl and season. Dip the chicken into the egg, let the excess drip back into the bowl, then press into the toasty breadcrumbs. Put under the grill on a flat baking sheet and grill for about 10 mins, turning once, until golden and crisp on both sides and the chicken is cooked through.

## STEP 3

Beat the lemon zest, juice and lots of black pepper into the mayonnaise. Spread some of the mayo onto the bottom halves of the buns, top with a chicken breast and salad of your choice and serve.

# Courgette lasagne

**Prep:** 20 mins **Cook:** 1 hr and 25 mins

**Serves 6**

## Ingredients

- 8 plum tomatoes , halved
- 2 garlic cloves , lightly bashed
- 1 tbsp olive oil
- 1 rosemary sprig
- ½ tbsp golden caster sugar
- 2 leeks , sliced into rings
- 20g unsalted butter
- 100g baby spinach
- 500g courgettes , grated
- 10 lasagne sheets
- 250g tub of ricotta
- 125g mozzarella , torn
- 50g parmesan (or vegetarian alternative), grated

**Method**

**STEP 1**

Heat oven to 200C/180C fan/gas 6. Put the tomatoes on a baking tray with the garlic, oil, rosemary and a good pinch of seasoning. Bake for 25-30 mins until soft, then discard the rosemary and peel off the garlic skin. Put the tomatoes, garlic and sugar in a blender and blitz a few times until you have a chunky sauce.

**STEP 2**

Meanwhile, put the leeks in a pan over a low heat, add the butter, season and cook for 7-10 mins or until soft. Add the spinach and courgettes, and cook, covered, for 2 mins until wilted and soft. Set aside.

## STEP 3

In a lasagne dish, layer up the ingredients using the tomato sauce first, then some pasta, followed by the ricotta and vegetables. Keep layering until you've used up everything. Finish with a final layer of the vegetables, the mozzarella and the Parmesan. Bake in the oven for 40-45 mins until the sauce has reduced and the top is golden brown.

# Pea & feta pearl barley stew

**Prep:** 10 mins **Cook:** 45 mins

**Serves 4**

# Ingredients

- 2 tbsp olive oil
- 2 medium onions , chopped
- 2 garlic cloves , chopped
- zest and juice 2 lemons
- 200g pearl barley , rinsed under cold water
- 700ml vegetable stock
- 200g feta , cut into cubes
- ½ small pack mint , leaves shredded, plus a few whole leaves to serve
- 400g frozen peas , defrosted at room temperature

**Method**

## STEP 1

Heat 1 tbsp oil in a pan or flameproof casserole dish over a medium heat. Add the onion and cook for 3 mins, then add the garlic and lemon zest and fry for another 1 min. Add the pearl barley and the stock. Season, bring to the boil, then simmer for 30 mins, stirring occasionally.

## STEP 2

Meanwhile, put the feta in a bowl with the remaining olive oil, half the lemon juice, most of the mint and a good grinding of black pepper. Leave to marinate while the barley cooks.

## STEP 3

Remove the lid from the barley and cook for 5 mins more. Increase the heat then add the peas, half the feta and all the feta juices. Cook for 3 mins, then check the seasoning. Divide between four bowls and top with the remaining feta and mint.

# Veggie olive wraps with mustard vinaigrette

**Prep:** 10 mins no cook

**Serves 1**

## Ingredients

- 1 carrot , shredded or coarsely grated
- 80g wedge red cabbage , finely shredded
- 2 spring onions , thinly sliced
- 1 courgette , shredded or coarsely grated
- handful basil leaves
- 5 green olives , pitted and halved
- ½ tsp English mustard powder
- 2 tsp extra virgin rapeseed oil
- 1 tbsp cider vinegar
- 1 large seeded tortilla

**Method**

**STEP 1**

Mix all the ingredients except for the tortilla and toss well.

**STEP 2**

Put the tortilla on a sheet of foil and pile the filling along one side of the wrap – it will almost look like too much mixture, but once you start to roll it firmly it will compact. Roll the tortilla from the filling side, folding in the sides as you go. Fold the foil in at the ends to keep stuff inside the wrap. Cut in half and eat straight away. If taking to work, leave whole and wrap up like a cracker in baking parchment.

# Cucumber, pea & lettuce soup

**Prep:** 5 mins **Cook:** 15 mins

**Serves 4**

# Ingredients

- 1 tsp rapeseed oil
- small bunch spring onions , roughly chopped
- 1 cucumber , roughly chopped
- 1 large round lettuce , roughly chopped
- 225g frozen peas
- 4 tsp vegetable bouillon
- 4 tbsp bio yogurt (optional)
- 4 slices rye bread

## Method

### STEP 1

Boil 1.4 litres water in a kettle. Heat the oil in a large non-stick frying pan and cook the spring onions for 5 mins, stirring frequently, or until softened. Add the cucumber, lettuce and peas, then pour in the boiled water. Stir in the bouillon, cover and simmer for 10 mins or until the vegetables are soft but still bright green.

### STEP 2

Blitz the mixture with a hand blender until smooth. Serve hot or cold, topped with yogurt (if you like), with rye bread alongside.

# Mexican rice & bean salad

**Prep:** 20 mins **Cook:** 15 mins

**Serves 4**

# Ingredients

- 175g/6oz basmati and wild rice
- 400g can mixed bean salad , drained and rinsed
- bunch spring onions , chopped
- 1 red pepper , deseeded and chopped
- 1 avocado , chopped

- juice 1 lime , plus wedges to serve
- 1 tbsp Cajun spice mix
- small bunch coriander , chopped

**Method**

**STEP 1**

Cook the rice following pack instructions. Drain, then cool under cold running water until completely cold. Stir in beans, onions, pepper and avocado.

**STEP 2**

Mix the lime juice with the Cajun spice mix and some black pepper. Pour over the rice mix, stir in the coriander and serve with extra lime wedges.

# Thin-stemmed broccoli with hoisin sauce & fried shallots

**Prep:**5 mins **Cook:**15 mins

**Serves 8**

## Ingredients

- vegetable oil , for shallow frying
- 4 shallots , thinly sliced
- 1 garlic clove , thinly sliced
- 500g thin-stemmed broccoli
- 4 tbsp hoisin sauce

**Method**

**STEP 1**

Heat 2.5cm of oil in a small saucepan until a small piece of bread sizzles. Add the shallots and garlic, and fry for about 2 mins or until golden. Drain on kitchen paper and sprinkle with salt.

**STEP 2**

Bring a large pan of water to the boil. Add the broccoli and blanch for 5-10 mins until just cooked, then drain. Serve immediately on a large platter drizzled with the hoisin sauce and sprinkled with the fried garlic and shallots.

# Rich paprika seafood bowl

**Prep:**10 mins **Cook:**20 mins

**Serves 4**

## Ingredients

- 1 tbsp olive oil
- 2 onions , halved and thinly sliced
- 2 celery stalks, finely chopped
- large bunch flat-leaf parsley , leaves and stalks separated
- 2-3 tsp paprika
- 200g roasted red pepper , drained weight, thickly sliced
- 400g can chopped tomato with garlic
- 400g white fish fillet, cut into very large chunks
- few fresh mussels (optional)

## Method

### STEP 1

Heat the oil in a pan, then add the onions, celery and a little salt. Cover, then gently fry until soft, about 10 mins. Put the parsley stalks, half the leaves, oil and seasoning into a food processor and whizz to a paste. Add this and the paprika to the softened onions, frying for a few mins. Tip in the peppers and tomatoes with a splash of water, then simmer for 10 mins until the sauce has reduced.

### STEP 2

Lay the fish and mussels on top of the sauce, put a lid on, then simmer for 5 mins until the fish is just flaking and the mussels have opened – discard any that stay shut. Gently stir the seafood into the sauce, season, then serve in bowls.

# One-pan prawn & tomato curry

**Prep:**10 mins **Cook:**20 mins

**Serves 4**

# Ingredients

- 2 tbsp sunflower oil
- 1 large onion , chopped
- large piece ginger , crushed
- 4 garlic cloves , crushed
- ½ red chilli , finely chopped
- 1 tsp golden caster sugar
- 1 tsp black mustard seeds
- 1 tsp ground cumin
- 1 tsp ground coriander
- 1 tsp turmeric
- 1 tbsp garam masala
- 2 tsp malt vinegar
- 400g can chopped tomato
- 400g raw king prawns
- small bunch coriander , chopped
- basmati rice , yogurt, mango chutney and Carrot & cumin salad, to serve

**Method**

**STEP 1**

Heat the oil in a deep-sided frying pan and cook the onion for 8-10 mins until it starts to turn golden. Add the ginger, garlic and chilli and cook for 1-2 mins. Stir in the sugar and spices for 1 min, then splash in the vinegar and tomatoes. Season with salt and simmer for 5 mins, stirring, until the sauce thickens.

**STEP 2**

Stir in the prawns, reduce the heat and cook for 8-10 mins until cooked through – if the sauce gets really thick, add a splash of water. Remove from the heat, stir though most of the coriander. Serve straight from the dish scattered with the remaining coriander and the rice, yogurt, chutney and salad in separate bowls.

# Easy Thai beef salad

**Prep:**15 mins **Cook:**5 mins Plus resting

**Serves 2**

## Ingredients

- 300g rump steak , trimmed of fat
- 2 tsp groundnut oil
- juice 1 lime
- 1 red chilli , deseeded and sliced (bird's-eye chillies work well)
- 1 tbsp light brown soft sugar
- 85g bag baby leaf salad
- 140g beansprouts
- 140g red grapes , halved
- steamed rice , to serve (optional)

**Method**

**STEP 1**

Rub the steak with 1 tsp oil and season. Fry in a hot pan for 2-2½ mins each side (depending on thickness), for medium rare. Transfer to a plate, cover loosely with foil and rest for 5 mins.

**STEP 2**

Make the dressing by mixing the lime juice, chilli, sugar and remaining oil in a bowl. Set aside until the sugar dissolves.

**STEP 3**

Divide the salad leaves, beansprouts and grapes between 2 serving bowls. Thinly slice the steak and add the juices to the dressing. Drizzle this over the salads, toss with the sliced beef and serve immediately with rice, if you like.

# Penne with broccoli, lemon & anchovies

**Prep:**10 mins **Cook:**17 mins

**Serves 2**

## Ingredients

- 170g wholemeal penne
- 1 leek , washed and sliced
- 180g broccoli , cut into small florets
- 2 tsp oil from the anchovy can, plus 15g anchovies, chopped
- 1 red pepper , seeded, quartered and sliced
- ½ tsp finely chopped rosemary
- 1 red chilli , seeded and sliced
- 3 garlic cloves , sliced
- ½ lemon , zested and juiced
- 4 tbsp ricotta
- 2 tbsp sunflower seeds

### Method

### STEP 1

Boil the pasta with the sliced leek for 7 mins, then add the broccoli and boil for 5 mins until everything is just tender.

### STEP 2

Meanwhile, heat the oil from the anchovies and fry the red pepper with the rosemary, chilli and garlic in a large non-stick pan for 5 mins until softened.

### STEP 3

Drain the pasta, reserving a little water, then tip the pasta and veg into the pan and add the lemon juice and zest, anchovies and ricotta. Toss well over the heat, using the pasta water to moisten. Toss through the sunflower seeds and serve.

# Walnut & almond muesli with grated apple

**Prep:**10 mins **Cook:**2 mins

**Serves 4**

## Ingredients

- 85g porridge oats

- 15g flaked almonds
- 15g walnut pieces
- 15g pumpkin seeds
- 1 tsp ground cinnamon
- 80g raisins
- 15g high fibre puffed wheat (we used Good Grain)
- 4 apples , no need to peel, grated
- milk , to serve

## Method

### STEP 1

Put the porridge oats in a saucepan and heat gently, stirring frequently until they're just starting to toast. Turn off the heat, then add all of the nuts, pumpkin seeds, and cinnamon, then stir everything together well.

### STEP 2

Tip into a large bowl, stir to help it cool, then add the raisins and puffed wheat and toss together until well mixed. Tip half into a jar or airtight container and save for another day – it will keep at room temperature. Serve the rest in two bowls, grate over 2 apples and pour over some cold milk (use nut milk if you're vegan) at the table. Save the other apples for the remaining muesli.

# Lemony prawn pasta

**Prep:**10 mins **Cook:**15 mins

**Serves 4**

# Ingredients

- 300g short pasta shapes
- 1 head broccoli , cut into small florets
- 200g large cooked prawns , halved
- 3 tbsp crème fraîche or double cream
- juice ½ lemon

## Method

### STEP 1

Cook the pasta following pack instructions, scooping out a bit of the cooking water as it cooks. Three mins before the pasta is done, add the broccoli to the pan and cook for the 3 mins more. Drain, then tip back into the pan.

## STEP 2

Reduce the heat to very low and gently stir through the prawns, crème fraîche, lemon juice and some seasoning. Add a splash of the reserved pasta water if it looks too thick, then serve when everything is really hot.

# Minced beef cobbler

**Prep:** 20 mins **Cook:** 50 mins

**Serves 4**

# Ingredients

- 500g pack extra-lean beef mince
- 1 onion , finely chopped
- 140g baby chestnut mushroom , halved
- 2 tbsp plain flour
- 500ml beef stock
- few shakes Worcestershire sauce
- 140g self-raising flour
- 1 tbsp chopped thyme
- 4 tbsp low-fat natural yogurt
- 140g frozen peas

**Method**

**STEP 1**

Heat oven to 180C/160C fan/gas 4. Dry-fry the mince and onion in a large non-stick frying pan over a high heat. Stir frequently to break up the mince, until well browned. Add the mushrooms and plain flour, followed by the stock and Worcestershire sauce. Bring to a simmer, then gently cook for 10 mins.

**STEP 2**

Meanwhile, to make the cobbles, mix the self-raising flour and thyme together in a bowl. Stir in the yogurt with enough cold water to form a scone-like dough. On a lightly floured surface, roll out to the thickness of about 1.5cm and use a cutter to stamp out 12 x 5cm rounds.

## STEP 3

Stir the peas into the mince mixture, then transfer to a baking dish. Randomly place the cobbles on top of the mince, then bake for 20-25 mins, until cobbles are risen and golden brown. This is good served with horseradish sauce.

# Tasty cottage pie with parsnip mash

**Prep:**1 hr and 15 mins **Cook:**30 mins

**Serves 4**

# Ingredients

- 250g packet lean minced beef (12% fat)
- 2 onions , chopped
- 4 carrots (about 450g/1lb), peeled and coarsely grated
- 2 tbsp Worcestershire sauce
- 2 tbsp tomato purée
- 2 beef stock , cubes dissolved in 425ml/¾pint boiling water
- 1 tsp cornflour
- 900g potato , peeled and cubed
- 3 parsnips , peeled, cored and chopped
- 2-4 tbsp skimmed milk
- steamed broccoli or Savoy cabbage to serve

**Method**

## STEP 1

Dry fry the mince (without adding any oil) in a non-stick pan until evenly brown and crumbly. Add the onions and carrots and cook over a high heat for 5 minutes, stirring well.

## STEP 2

Add the Worcestershire sauce and tomato purée, pour in the stock and bring to the boil, stirring until well mixed. Cover the pan and leave to simmer for 40 minutes, stirring occasionally until the carrots and onions are tender and the stock has reduced. Taste and season. Blend the cornflour with a little water and stir into the mixture, cooking for a minute or until slightly thickened.

## STEP 3

Preheat the oven to 200C/Gas 6/ fan oven 180C. While the meat is simmering, cook the potatoes and parsnips in boiling salted water for 15 minutes or until tender. Drain and mash with seasoning and enough milk to make a creamy consistency.

## STEP 4

Tip the meat mixture into a 1.4 litre/ 2½ pint ovenproof dish, spoon the mash on top and rough up the surface with a fork. Bake for 30 minutes or until the potato topping is lightly golden. Serve with steamed broccoli or Savoy cabbage.

# Turkey & spring onion wraps

**Prep:**5 mins No cook

**Serves 4**

## Ingredients

- 2 tbsp reduced-fat mayonnaise
- 2 tbsp pesto
- 4 curly lettuce leaves
- 250g cooked turkey , shredded
- 6 spring onions , shredded
- 12cm chunk cucumber ,shredded
- 4 flour tortillas

**Method**

## STEP 1

Mix together the mayonnaise and pesto. Divide the lettuce leaves, turkey, spring onions and cucumber between the tortillas. Drizzle over the pesto dressing, roll up and eat.

# Lighter chicken tacos

**Prep:**35 mins **Cook:**25 mins

**Serves 4**

# Ingredients

### For the chicken

- 2 tsp rapeseed oil
- 1 tsp ground cumin
- 1 tsp smoked paprika
- 450g skinless chicken breasts, preferably organic

### For the salsa

- 4 medium tomatoes, preferably on the vine, halved
- 1 red pepper, quartered
- 1 small red onion, cut into 8 wedges
- ¼ tsp rapeseed oil
- 2 tsp lime juice
- ¼ tsp ground cumin
- good pinch of chilli flakes

### For the guacamole

- 2 medium-sized ripe avocados, stoned, peeled and roughly chopped
- 4 tsp lime juice
- 2 spring onions, ends trimmed, finely chopped
- 3 tbsp chopped coriander
- good pinch of chilli flakes

### To serve

- 8 corn tacos shells
- 8 tsp 0% Greek yogurt
- 2 Little Gem lettuces, shredded
- chopped coriander
- lime wedges, for squeezing over

### Method

**STEP 1**

Mix the oil with the cumin and paprika on a large plate. Sit the chicken on the plate and rub the spiced oil all over it. Season with pepper and a pinch of salt, then cover and set aside while you prepare the salsa.

**STEP 2**

Heat the grill to high for 10 mins. Meanwhile, line a large baking tray with foil and lay the tomatoes (cut-side up) on it, along with the pepper and red onion. Brush the oil over the onion, and season the tomatoes and onion with pepper. Grill for 12-15 mins, turning the tomatoes and onion halfway through, until well charred. Remove (leaving the grill on) and set aside to cool – put the pepper in a bowl and cover with cling film so that it's easier to skin later.

**STEP 3**

For the guacamole, put the avocado in a bowl and briefly mash with a fork, leaving some chunky pieces for texture. Gently mix in the lime juice, spring onions, coriander and chilli flakes. Season with pepper and a pinch of salt.

**STEP 4**

Re-line the baking tray with foil and lay the chicken on it, plump-side up. Grill for about 10 mins until cooked – there is no need to turn it. Meanwhile, scoop out and discard as much of the seeds and juice from the tomatoes as you can (so the salsa isn't too wet), leaving the pulp and charred skin. When the pepper is cool enough to handle, peel off and discard the skin. Chop the tomatoes and onion, and dice the pepper. Combine in a bowl with the lime juice, cumin, chilli flakes, some pepper and a pinch of salt.

**STEP 5**

When the chicken is cooked, remove from the grill, cover loosely with foil and set aside for 5 mins.

**STEP 6**

Heat oven to 180C/160C fan/gas 4. Cut the chicken into chunky slices and spoon over the juices. When ready to serve, lay the taco shells on a baking sheet and warm through for 2-3 mins. Serve the chicken, taco shells, yogurt, lettuce, coriander and lime wedges in separate bowls, so that everyone can build their own tacos.

# Chicken & broccoli potato-topped pie

**Prep:**35 mins **Cook:**1 hr and 25 mins

**Serves 4**

# Ingredients

- 750g potatoes, peeled and halved
- 250g broccoli, cut into small florets
- 100ml strong chicken stock
- small bunch tarragon, finely chopped (optional)
- 1-2 tsp Dijon mustard
- 100g frozen peas
- 1 tbsp butter

**For the chicken base**

- 25g butter
- 25g plain flour
- 250ml milk
- 1 tsp olive oil
- 2-3 (depending on size) skinless chicken thigh fillets, cut into cubes
- 1 skinless chicken breast, cut into cubes
- ⅓ onion, very finely chopped (optional)

**Method**

**STEP 1**

For the base, melt the butter in a saucepan, stir in the flour and cook for a few mins, stirring all the time. Now, using a whisk or spatula, carefully stir in the milk, a little at a time, making sure the sauce stays smooth. Bring the mixture to a simmer and cook for a couple of mins until it thickens – it will be very thick. Turn the heat right down and keep cooking for 5 mins, stirring often.

**STEP 2**

Meanwhile, heat the oil in a non-stick frying pan and fry all of the chicken in batches until it starts to colour lightly at the edges. Scoop out each batch of chicken and put it on a plate. Add the onion to the pan if you are using it, and cook over a low heat until soft. Add the chicken and any juices and the onion to the white sauce, fold it in and cook the mixture for a further 15 mins or until the chicken is cooked through. If you're making the base ahead of time, you can leave it to cool at this stage then freeze in an airtight container for up to a month. (Defrost fully before using in the next step.)

**STEP 3**

Heat oven to 180C/160C fan/gas 4. Cook the potatoes in boiling water for 10 mins, then drain and cool a little before slicing thickly.

**STEP 4**

Meanwhile, cook the broccoli until tender, then drain. Heat the chicken base with the stock in a pan until it is just beginning to bubble, then stir in the tarragon (if using) and the mustard. Fold in the broccoli and peas. Tip the chicken mixture into a dish and arrange the potato slices on top, then dot the butter over. Bake for 30-35 mins or until golden.

# Chinese chicken noodle soup with peanut sauce

**Prep:**15 mins **Cook:**30 mins

**Serves 2**

## Ingredients

- 1 tbsp sunflower oil
- 4 skinless boneless chicken thighs
- 1 garlic clove , crushed
- 1 thumb-sized piece ginger , grated
- 500ml chicken stock
- 1 tsp soy sauce
- ½ hispi cabbage , finely sliced
- 150g mushrooms
- 150g straight to wok noodles (we used udon)

**For the peanut sauce**

- 1 tbsp peanut butter
- 1 tsp soy sauce
- 1 tsp honey
- sriracha or other chilli sauce (optional), to serve

**Method**

**STEP 1**

Heat the oil in a saucepan over a medium heat, add the chicken and brown a little, so around 2-3 mins, then add the garlic and ginger and stir to coat the chicken. Fry for a further minute, then pour in the chicken stock and soy, bring to the boil, then reduce to a simmer. Cover with a lid and leave to gently bubble for 25-30 mins until the chicken is tender and pulls apart.

**STEP 2**

Meanwhile, mix the sauce ingredients with a splash of water. When the chicken is ready, lift it out with a slotted spoon and use two forks to shred it on a plate. Add the cabbage, mushrooms and noodles to the pan, turn up the heat, then stir in the chicken, add a dash of sriracha, if using, and ladle into bowls. Top with a drizzle of the peanut sauce and serve.

# Crab & lemon spaghetti with peas

**Prep:**7 mins **Cook:**12 mins

**Serves 2**

# Ingredients

- 150g wholemeal spaghetti
- 1 tbsp rapeseed oil
- 2 leeks (220g), cut into lengths then long thin strips
- 1 red chilli , deseeded and finely chopped
- 1 garlic clove , finely grated
- 160g frozen peas
- 1 lemon , zested and 1/2 juiced
- 100g fresh white and brown crabmeat (not dressed)

**Method**

**STEP 1**

Cook the spaghetti for 12 mins, or following pack instructions, until al dente. Meanwhile, heat the oil in a large frying pan, add the leeks and chilli and cook for 5 mins. Stir in the garlic, peas, lemon zest and juice, then cook for a few mins.

**STEP 2**

Drain the pasta, then add to the pan with ¼ mug of pasta water and the crab, then toss everything together until well coated. Spoon into shallow bowls and serve.

# Apple pie samosas

**Prep:** 20 mins **Cook:** 25 mins

**Serves 4**

## Ingredients

- 2 cooking apples , peeled, cored and chopped
- 50g caster sugar
- 1 tsp ground mixed spice
- 50g sultanas
- 4 sheets filo pastry
- 25g low-fat spread (we used Flora Light), melted

**Method**

**STEP 1**

Heat oven to 200C/180C fan/gas 6. Place the apples, sugar, mixed spice and sultanas in a saucepan with 2 tbsp water and cook, covered, for 6 mins or until the apples are soft, stirring once or twice. Tip into a shallow dish and spread out to cool slightly.

**STEP 2**

Cut the sheets of filo in thirds lengthways, then brush lightly with the melted spread. Place a spoonful of the apple filling at the top of each strip, then fold over and over to form triangular parcels. Place on a baking sheet and bake for 15-20 mins until crisp and golden. Serve with low-fat yogurt, if you like.

# Banana pancakes

**Prep:** 5 mins **Cook:** 5 mins

**Serves 2 (makes 4)**

## Ingredients

- 1 large banana
- 2 medium eggs, beaten
- pinch of baking powder (gluten-free if coeliac)
- splash of vanilla extract
- 1 tsp oil
- 25g pecans, roughly chopped
- 125g raspberries

**Method**

## STEP 1

In a bowl, mash 1 large banana with a fork until it resembles a thick purée.

## STEP 2

Stir in 2 beaten eggs, a pinch of baking powder (gluten-free if coeliac) and a splash of vanilla extract.

## STEP 3

Heat a large non-stick frying pan or pancake pan over a medium heat and brush with ½ tsp oil.

## STEP 4

Using half the batter, spoon two pancakes into the pan, cook for 1-2 mins each side, then tip onto a plate. Repeat the process with another ½ tsp oil and the remaining batter.

## STEP 5

Top the pancakes with 25g roughly chopped pecans and 125g raspberries.

# Green eggs

**Prep:**5 mins **Cook:**15 mins

**Serves 2**

# Ingredients

- 1½ tbsp rapeseed oil , plus a splash extra
- 2 trimmed leeks , sliced
- 2 garlic cloves , sliced

- ½ tsp coriander seeds
- ½ tsp fennel seeds
- pinch of chilli flakes , plus extra to serve
- 200g spinach
- 2 large eggs
- 2 tbsp Greek yogurt
- squeeze of lemon

**Method**

**STEP 1**

Heat the oil in a large frying pan. Add the leeks and a pinch of salt, then cook until soft. Add the garlic, coriander, fennel and chilli flakes. Once the seeds begin to crackle, tip in the spinach and turn down the heat. Stir everything together until the spinach has wilted and reduced, then scrape it over to one side of the pan. Pour a little oil into the pan, then crack in the eggs and fry until cooked to your liking.

**STEP 2**

Stir the yogurt through the spinach mix and season. Pile onto two plates, top with the fried egg, squeeze over a little lemon and season with black pepper and chilli flakes to serve.

# Roast pork with couscous & ginger yogurt

**Prep:** 10 mins **Cook:** 40 mins

**Serves 6**

# Ingredients

- 2 pork fillets , each about 500g/1lb 2oz, trimmed of any fat
- 2 tsp olive oil
- 3 tsp ground cumin
- 1 tsp ground cinnamon
- 4 tsp grated ginger
- 250g couscous
- 100g sultanas
- zest and juice 1 lemon
- small bunch mint , chopped

- 200g fat-free natural yogurt

**Method**

## STEP 1

Heat oven to 190C/170C fan/gas 5. Brown the pork in a non-stick frying pan over a high heat for 4-5 mins, turning twice. Mix the oil, 2 tsp cumin, cinnamon, 2 tsp ginger and some seasoning, then rub all over the pork. Transfer to a roasting tin and roast for 30-35 mins or until the juices run clear when the thickest part is pierced with a skewer.

## STEP 2

Mix the couscous with the remaining cumin, the sultanas, lemon zest and juice, then season and pour over 400ml boiling water. Stir well and cover for 5 mins, then stir in the mint.

## STEP 3

Stir the remaining ginger and a little seasoning into the yogurt. Thickly slice the pork and serve with the couscous and ginger yogurt.

# Lamb & squash biryani with cucumber raita

**Prep:** 10 mins **Cook:** 25 mins

**Serves 4**

# Ingredients

- 4 lean lamb steaks (about 400g), trimmed of all fat, cut into chunks
- 2 garlic cloves , finely grated
- 8 tsp chopped fresh ginger
- 3 tsp ground coriander
- 4 tsp rapeseed oil
- 4 onions , sliced
- 2 red chillies , deseeded and chopped
- 170g brown basmati rice
- 320g diced butternut squash
- 2 tsp cumin seeds
- 2 tsp vegetable bouillon powder
- 20cm length cucumber , grated

- 100ml bio yogurt
- 4 tbsp chopped mint , plus a few extra leaves
- handful coriander , chopped

**Method**

**STEP 1**

Mix the lamb with the garlic, 2 tsp chopped ginger and 1 tsp ground coriander and set aside.

**STEP 2**

Heat 2 tsp oil in a non-stick pan. Add the onions, the remaining ginger and chilli and stir-fry briefly over a high heat so they start to soften. Add the rice and squash and stir over the heat for a few mins. Tip in all the remaining spices, then stir in 500ml boiling water and the bouillon. Cover the pan and simmer for 20 mins.

**STEP 3**

Meanwhile, mix the cucumber, yogurt and mint together in a bowl to make a raita. Chill half for later.

**STEP 4**

About 5 mins before the rice is ready, heat the remaining oil in a non-stick frying pan, add the lamb and stir for a few mins until browned but still nice tender. Toss into the spiced rice with the coriander and serve with the raita and a few mint or coriander leaves on top.

# Roasted red pepper & tomato soup with ricotta

**Prep:**10 mins **Cook:**30 mins

**Serves 2**

## Ingredients

- 400g tomatoes , halved
- 1 red onion , quartered
- 2 Romano peppers , roughly chopped
- 2 tbsp good quality olive oil
- 2 garlic cloves , bashed in their skins
- few thyme sprigs

- 1 tbsp red wine vinegar
- 2 tbsp ricotta
- few basil leaves
- 1 tbsp mixed seeds , toasted
- bread , to serve

## Method

### STEP 1

Heat oven to 200C/180C fan/gas 6. Put the tomatoes, onion and peppers in a roasting tin, toss with the oil and season. Nestle in the garlic and thyme sprigs, then roast for 25-30 mins until all the veg has softened and slightly caramelised. Squeeze the garlic cloves out of their skins into the tin, strip the leaves off the thyme and discard the stalks and garlic skins. Mix the vinegar into the tin then blend everything in a bullet blender or using a stick blender, adding enough water to loosen to your preferred consistency (we used around 150ml).

### STEP 2

Reheat the soup if necessary, taste for seasoning, then spoon into two bowls and top each with a spoonful of ricotta, a few basil leaves, the seeds and a drizzle of oil. Serve with bread for dunking.

# Creamy yogurt porridge

**Prep:**1 min **Cook:**3 mins

**Serves 1**

## Ingredients

- 3 tbsp (25g) porridge oat
- 150g pot 0% fat probiotic yogurt

## Method

### STEP 1

Tip 200ml water into a small non-stick pan and stir in porridge oats.

### STEP 2

Cook over a low heat until bubbling and thickened. (To make in a microwave, use a deep container to prevent spillage as the mixture will rise up as it cooks, and cook for 3 mins on High.)

**STEP 3**

Stir in yogurt – or swirl in half and top with the rest. Serve plain or with one of our toppings (see 'goes well with').

# Noodles with turkey, green beans & hoisin

**Prep:** 10 mins **Cook:** 15 mins

**Serves 2**

## Ingredients

- 100g ramen noodles
- 100g green beans , halved
- 3 tbsp hoisin sauce
- juice 1 lime
- 1 tbsp chilli sauce
- 1 tbsp vegetable oil
- 250g turkey mince
- 2 garlic cloves , chopped
- 6 spring onions , sliced diagonally

**Method**

**STEP 1**

Boil the noodles following pack instructions, adding the green beans for the final 2 mins. Drain and set aside.

**STEP 2**

In a small bowl, mix together the hoisin, lime juice and chilli sauce. In a wok or frying pan, heat the oil, then fry the mince until nicely browned. Add the garlic and fry for 1 min more. Stir in the hoisin mixture and cook for a few mins more until sticky. Finally, stir in the noodles, beans and half the spring onions to heat through. Scatter over the remaining spring onions to serve.

# Ginger & soy sea bass parcels

**Prep:**30 mins **Cook:**15 mins

**Serves 4**

# Ingredients

- 100ml shaohsing rice wine or dry sherry
- 100ml light soy sauce
- 1 small bunch of spring onions , finely sliced
- 2 garlic cloves , finely chopped
- thumb-sized piece fresh ginger , finely chopped
- 4 sea bass fillets, scaled (about 100g each)
- 3 pak choi , each quartered
- 1 large carrot , shredded into fine strips
- 2 red chillies , 4 spring onions, and thumb-sized piece ginger, cut into fine strips, to serve

**Method**

**STEP 1**

In a jug, mix together the wine or sherry with the soy, spring onions, garlic and ginger, then set aside. Lightly score the skin of each sea bass fillet a couple of times.

**STEP 2**

Lay a square of foil on your work surface with a square of baking parchment the same size on top. Put 3 pak choi quarters just off centre of the paper and top with a quarter of the shredded carrot followed by a sea bass fillet, skin-side up. Spoon over a quarter of the ginger, onion and garlic mixture (don't add the rice wine and soy mixture yet). Fold over the parcel so it becomes a triangle, then, from left to right, begin to seal it by scrunching the edges together. Continue all the way around until there is just a little hole at the end. Pour a quarter of the soy mix through the hole. Scrunch the remaining bit to seal and place on a baking tray. Repeat until all the fish are wrapped, sauced and sealed. Can be prepared a day ahead and chilled.

**STEP 3**

Heat oven to 200C/180C fan/gas 6 and cook the fish on the tray for 15 mins. Remove from the oven and divide the parcels between four warmed plates. Let your guests open them up themselves so they get a hit of aromatic steam before they tuck in. Pass around some chilli, spring onion and ginger strips to sprinkle over.

# Vegetarian bean pot with herby breadcrumbs

**Prep:**10 mins **Cook:**35 mins

**Serves 2**

## Ingredients

- 1 slice crusty bread
- ½ small pack parsley leaves
- ½ lemon , zested
- 2 tbsp olive oil
- pinch chilli flakes (optional)
- 2 leeks , rinsed and chopped into half-moons
- 2 carrots , thinly sliced
- 2 celery sticks , thinly sliced
- 1 fennel bulb , thinly sliced
- 2 large garlic cloves , chopped
- 1 tbsp tomato purée
- few thyme sprigs
- 150ml white wine
- 400g can cannellini beans , drained

**Method**

**STEP 1**

Toast the bread, then tear into pieces and put in a food processor with the parsley, lemon zest, ½ tbsp olive oil, a good pinch of salt and pepper and the chilli flakes, if using. Blitz to breadcrumbs. Set aside.

**STEP 2**

Heat the remaining oil in a pan and add the leeks, carrots, celery and fennel along with a splash of water and a pinch of salt. Cook over a medium heat for 10 mins until soft, then add the garlic and tomato purée. Cook for 1 min more, then add the thyme and white wine. Leave to bubble for a minute, then add the beans. Fill the can halfway with water and pour into the pot.

**STEP 3**

Bring the cassoulet to the boil, then turn down the heat and leave to simmer for 15 mins before removing the thyme sprigs. Mash half the beans to thicken the stew. Season to taste, then divide between bowls and top with the herby breadcrumbs to serve.

# Savoy cabbage with shallots & fennel seeds

**Prep:**20 mins **Cook:**30 mins

**Serves 8**

# Ingredients

- 300g pack small shallots
- 2 tbsp olive oil
- 2 large garlic cloves , sliced
- 1 tsp fennel seeds , lightly crushed
- 1 Savoy cabbage (outer leaves discarded) quartered, cored and shredded
- 150ml hot vegetable stock

**Method**

**STEP 1**

Boil the shallots in their skins for 10-15 mins until they are soft but still hold their shape. Leave to cool then slip the skins from the shallots and halve them. Can be prepared a couple of days in advance, then chilled.

**STEP 2**

Heat the oil in a large non-stick wok, and stir-fry the garlic, fennel seeds and shallots for a couple of mins until the shallots are golden. Remove from the pan.

**STEP 3**

Add the cabbage to the pan and stir-fry until it starts to wilt a little, then pour in the stock, cover the wok and cook for 3 mins until just tender. Test to see if the cabbage is done to your liking; if not, cook a little longer, then add the shallot mixture, heat through and serve.

# Healthy salad Niçoise

**Prep:**15 mins **Cook:**10 mins

**Serves 2**

# Ingredients

- 200g new potato , thickly sliced
- 2 medium eggs
- 100g green bean , trimmed
- 1 romaine lettuce heart, leaves separated and washed
- 8 cherry tomatoes , halved
- 6 anchovies in olive oil, drained well
- 197g can tuna steak in spring water, drained
- 2 tbsp reduced-fat mayonnaise

**Method**

**STEP 1**

Bring a large pan of water to the boil. Add the potatoes and the eggs, and cook for 7 mins. Scoop the eggs out of the pan, tip in the green beans and cook for a further 4 mins. Drain the potatoes, beans and eggs in a colander under cold running water until cool. Leave to dry.

**STEP 2**

Peel the eggs and cut into quarters. Arrange the lettuce leaves in 2 shallow bowls. Scatter over the beans, potatoes, tomatoes and egg quarters. Pat the anchovies with kitchen paper to absorb the excess oil and place on top.

**STEP 3**

Flake the tuna into chunks and scatter over the salad. Mix the mayonnaise and 1 tbsp cold water in a bowl until smooth. Drizzle over the salad and serve.

# Mumbai potato wraps with minted yogurt relish

**Prep:**10 mins - 15 mins **Cook:**35 mins

**Serves 4**

# Ingredients

- 2 tsp sunflower oil
- 1 onion , sliced
- 2 tbsp medium curry powder
- 400g can chopped tomato
- 750g potato , diced
- 2 tbsp spiced mango chutney , plus extra to serve
- 100g low-fat natural yogurt
- 1 tsp mint sauce from a jar
- 8 small plain chapatis
- coriander sprigs, to serve

**Method**

**STEP 1**

Heat the sunflower oil in a large saucepan and fry the onion for 6-8 mins until golden and soft. Stir in 1½ tbsp curry powder, cook for 30 secs, then add the tomatoes and seasoning. Simmer, uncovered, for 15 mins.

**STEP 2**

Meanwhile, add the potatoes and ½ tbsp curry powder to a pan of boiling salted water. Cook for 6-8 mins until just tender. Drain, reserving 100ml of the liquid. Add the drained potatoes and reserved liquid to the tomato sauce along with the mango chutney. Heat through.

**STEP 3**

Meanwhile, mix together the yogurt and mint sauce, and warm the chapattis following pack instructions.

**STEP 4**

To serve, spoon some of the potatoes onto a chapatti and top with a few sprigs of coriander. Drizzle with the minted yogurt relish, adding extra mango chutney if you wish, then roll up and eat.

# Banana & cinnamon pancakes with blueberry compote

**Prep:**10 mins **Cook:**15 mins

**Serves 4**

## Ingredients

- 65g wholemeal flour
- 1 tsp ground cinnamon , plus extra for sprinkling
- 2 egg , plus 2 egg whites
- 100ml whole milk
- 1 small banana , mashed
- ½ tbsp rapeseed oil
- 320g blueberries
- few mint leaves , to serve

**Method**

**STEP 1**

Tip the flour and cinnamon into a bowl, then break in the whole eggs, pour in the milk and whisk together until smooth. Stir in the banana. In a separate bowl, whisk the egg whites until light and fluffy, but not completely stiff, then fold into the pancake mix until evenly incorporated.

**STEP 2**

Heat a small amount of oil in a large non-stick frying pan, then add a quarter of the pancake mix, swirl to cover the base of the pan and cook until set and golden. Carefully turn the pancake over with a palette knife and cook the other side. Transfer to a plate, then carry on with the rest of the batter until you have four.

**STEP 3**

To make the compote, tip the berries in a non-stick pan and heat gently until the berries just burst but hold their shape. Serve two warm pancakes with half the berries, then scatter with the mint leaves and sprinkle with a little cinnamon. Chill the remaining pancakes and compote and serve the next day. You can reheat them in the microwave or in a pan.

# 15-minute chicken pasta

**Cook:**15 mins **Serves 4**

## Ingredients

148

- 350g pasta bows (farfalle)
- 300g broccoli , cut into small florets
- 1 tbsp olive oil
- 3 large skinless boneless chicken breasts, cut into bite-sized chunks
- 2 garlic cloves , crushed
- 2 tbsp wholegrain mustard
- juice of 1 large or 2 small oranges
- 25g flaked almond , toasted

## Method

### STEP 1

Cook the pasta in plenty of boiling salted water according to the packet instructions. Three minutes before the pasta is cooked, throw the broccoli into the pasta water and continue to boil.

### STEP 2

While the pasta is cooking, gently heat the oil in a large frying pan or wok. Tip in the chicken and fry, stirring occasionally, until the chicken pieces are cooked and golden, about 8-10 minutes, adding the garlic for the last 2 minutes.

### STEP 3

Mix the mustard with the orange juice in a small bowl. Pour the mixture over the chicken, and gently simmer for a minute or two. Drain the pasta and broccoli, reserving 3 tablespoons of the pasta water. Toss the pasta and broccoli with the chicken, stir in the pasta water and the almonds, season well and serve.

# Easy turkey paella

Cook:18 mins - 24 mins **Serves 4**

# Ingredients

- 205g jar of paella paste
- 300g paella rice
- 300g pack stir-fry vegetables (without beansprouts)
- 130g pack roast turkey slices

## Method

## STEP 1

Heat 1 tbsp olive oil in a large sauté pan. Fry the paella paste for 1-2 mins, then tip in the rice and cook for 2 mins more. Add 800ml boiling water, simmer for 12-15 mins or until the liquid has been absorbed, then season to taste.

## STEP 2

In another pan, fry the veg in 1 tbsp olive oil on a high heat for 1-2 mins. Add 50ml water, cove and steam for 2-3 mins. Tear the turkey into bite-sized pieces and stir through the rice with the veg.

# Teriyaki prawns & broccoli noodles

**Prep:**10 mins **Cook:**10 mins

**Serves 2**

## Ingredients

- 50ml low-sodium soy sauce
- 50ml mirin
- 2 tbsp lemon juice
- 1 ½ tbsp caster sugar
- 200g soba noodle
- 140g thin-stemmed broccoli
- 140g cooked prawn
- 1 small red chilli , thinly sliced

**Method**

## STEP 1

In a small saucepan, heat the soy sauce, mirin, lemon juice and sugar. Simmer for 5 mins until syrupy, then remove from the heat. Bring a large saucepan of salted water to the boil, then cook the noodles and broccoli for about 3 mins, adding the prawns a few secs before draining. Divide the mixture between 2 plates, pour the warm teriyaki sauce over the top, sprinkle with the red chilli and serve.

# Spicy mince & lettuce cups

Prep:10 mins **Cook:**15 mins Ready in 25 minutes

Serves 4

# Ingredients

- 1 tbsp sunflower oil
- large piece fresh root ginger , peeled and grated
- 2 garlic cloves , crushed
- 2 red chillies , deseeded and finely sliced
- 500g minced chicken , turkey or pork
- 85g light brown sugar
- 2 tbsp fish sauce
- juice 1 lime
- 2 lime leaves , finely shredded

## To serve

- mix of iceberg lettuce , Little Gem and cos leaves
- large handful mint and coriander leaves, very roughly chopped
- handful toasted peanuts , roughly chopped
- 2 shallots , finely sliced into rings
- 1 lime , cut into wedges

## Method

### STEP 1

Heat the oil in a large frying pan. Fry the ginger, garlic and chillies for 1 min. Add the mince, then cook on a high heat until golden brown, breaking it up with a wooden spoon as you go. Sprinkle over the brown sugar, fish sauce, lime juice and shredded lime leaves, then cook everything down until sticky.

### STEP 2

Tip the mince into a serving bowl, then serve with a bowl of lettuce leaves for wrapping the mince in; the herbs, shallots and peanuts for scattering over; and the lime wedges for squeezing.

# Black-eyed bean mole with salsa

**Prep:**15 mins **Cook:**5 mins - 8 mins

**Serves 2**

## Ingredients

### For the salsa

- 1 red onion , finely chopped
- 2 large tomatoes , chopped
- 2 tbsp fresh coriander
- ½ lime , zest and juice

### For the mole

- 2 tsp rapeseed oil
- 1 red onion , halved and sliced
- 1 garlic clove , finely grated
- 1 tsp ground coriander
- 1 tsp mild chilli powder
- ½ tsp ground cinnamon
- 400g can black-eyed beans in water
- 2 tsp cocoa
- 1 tsp vegetable bouillon
- 1 tbsp tomato purée

### Method

### STEP 1

Tip all the salsa ingredients into a bowl and stir together.

### STEP 2

For the mole, heat the oil in a non-stick pan, add the onion and garlic and fry stirring frequently until softened. Tip in the spices, stir then add the contents of the can of beans with the cocoa, bouillon and tomato purée. Cook, stirring frequently to make quite a thick sauce.

### STEP 3

Spoon into shallow bowls, top with the salsa and serve.

# Avocado hummus & crudités

**Prep:**10 mins No cook

**Serves 2**

# Ingredients

- 1 avocado , peeled and stoned
- 210g chickpeas , drained
- 1 garlic clove , crushed
- pinch chilli flakes , plus extra to serve
- 1 lime , juiced
- handful coriander leaves
- 2 carrots , cut into strips
- 2 mixed peppers , cut into strips
- 160g sugar snap peas

**Method**

**STEP 1**

Blitz together the avocado, chickpeas, garlic, chilli flakes and lime juice, and season to taste. Top the hummus with the coriander leaves and a few more chilli flakes, and serve with the carrot, pepper and sugar snap crudités. Make the night before for a great take-to-work lunch.

# Breakfast super-shake

**Prep:**5 mins no cook

**Serves 1**

# Ingredients

- 100ml full-fat milk
- 2 tbsp natural yogurt
- 1 banana
- 150g frozen fruits of the forest
- 50g blueberries
- 1 tbsp chia seeds
- ½ tsp cinnamon
- 1 tbsp goji berries

- 1 tsp mixed seeds
- 1 tsp honey (ideally Manuka)

**Method**

**STEP 1**

Put the ingredients in a blender and blitz until smooth. Pour into a glass and enjoy!

# Avocado & strawberry ices

**Prep:** 5 mins Plus freezing

**Serves 4**

## Ingredients

- 200g ripe strawberries , hulled and chopped
- 1 avocado , stoned, peeled and roughly chopped
- 2 tsp balsamic vinegar
- ½ tsp vanilla extract
- 1-2 tsp maple syrup (optional)

## Method

**STEP 1**

Put the strawberries (save four pieces for the top), avocado, vinegar and vanilla in a bowl and blitz using a hand blender (or in a food processor) until as smooth as you can get it. Have a taste and only add the maple syrup if the strawberries are not sweet enough.

**STEP 2**

Pour into containers, add a strawberry to each, cover with cling film and freeze. Allow the pots to soften for 5-10 mins before eating.

# Salmon pasta salad with lemon & capers

**Prep:** 10 mins **Cook:** 20 mins

**Serves 2**

## Ingredients

- 85g wholewheat penne
- 1 tbsp rapeseed oil
- 1 large red pepper , roughly chopped
- 2 frozen, skinless wild salmon fillets (about 120g each)
- 1 lemon , zested and juiced
- 2 garlic cloves , finely grated
- 1 shallot , very finely chopped
- 2 tbsp capers
- 6 pitted Kalamata olives , sliced
- 1 tsp extra virgin olive oil
- 2 handfuls rocket

**Method**

**STEP 1**

Cook the pasta following pack instructions. Meanwhile, heat the rapeseed oil in a frying pan, add the pepper, cover and leave for about 5 mins until it softens and starts to char a little. Stir, then push the pepper to one side and add the salmon. Cover and fry for 8-10 mins until just cooked.

**STEP 2**

Meanwhile, mix the lemon zest and juice in a large bowl with the garlic, shallot, capers and olives.

**STEP 3**

Add the cooked pepper and salmon to the bowl. Drain the pasta and add it too, with black pepper and the olive oil. Toss everything together, flaking the salmon as you do so. If eating now, toss through the rocket; if packing a lunch, leave to cool, then put in a container with the rocket on top and mix through just before eating.

# Thai shredded chicken & runner bean salad

Prep:30 mins **Cook:**5 mins

**Serves 4**

## Ingredients

- 200g runner beans (or any other green bean), topped and tailed
- 1 red chilli , halved and finely sliced, use a bird's eye chilli for more heat
- 2 shallots , finely sliced
- 1 lemongrass , finely sliced
- 2cm piece ginger , shredded
- 2 cooked, skinless chicken breasts
- small bunch mint leaves
- large bunch Thai basil or coriander
- 1 lime cut in wedges or cheeks, to serve
- steamed jasmine rice , to serve

### Coconut dressing

- 100ml coconut cream
- 1 garlic clove , crushed
- 3 tbsp fish sauce
- 1 tsp sugar
- juice 1 lime
- 1 bird's eye chilli , finely diced

### Method

### STEP 1

Run a potato peeler down either side of the beans to remove any stringy bits. Cut into strips using a bean slicer, or on the diagonal into 2cm pieces. Cook the beans in simmering salted water for 4 mins or until tender but still bright green. Drain and put in a bowl with the chilli, shallots, lemongrass and ginger. Pull the chicken breasts into shreds using your fingers and add to the bowl.

### STEP 2

Make the dressing. Mix the coconut with the garlic, fish sauce, sugar, lime and chilli. Tear the mint and Thai basil over the chicken and toss everything together. Pile onto a plate and pour over the dressing. Serve with the lime to squeeze over and jasmine rice.

# Squash & chorizo stew

**Prep:**10 mins **Cook:**25 mins

**Serves 4**

# Ingredients

- 140g chorizo , thickly sliced
- 1 onion , chopped
- 680g jar passata
- 1 butternut squash (approx 1kg/2lb 4oz), peeled and cut into 1-2cm chunks
- flat-leaf parsley , chopped

**Method**

**STEP 1**

Heat a large pan, add the chorizo, then cook over a high heat for 2 mins until it starts to release its red oil. Lift the chorizo out of the pan, then add the onion and fry for 5 mins until starting to soften.

**STEP 2**

Tip in the passata, squash and chorizo, bring to the boil, then cover and cook for 15-20 mins until the squash is softened, but not broken up. If you need to, add a little water during cooking. Season to taste, then serve in bowls scattered with parsley.

# Miso steak

**Prep:**10 mins **Cook:**10 mins Plus marinating

**Serves 2**

# Ingredients

- 2 tbsp brown miso paste
- 1 tbsp dry sherry or sake
- 1 tbsp caster sugar
- 2 crushed garlic cloves
- 300g/11oz lean steak
- baby spinach , sliced cucumber, celery, radish and toasted sesame seeds, to serve

**Method**

**STEP 1**

Tip the miso paste, Sherry or sake, sugar and garlic into a sealable food bag. Season with a generous grinding of black pepper, then squash it all together until completely mixed. Add the steak, gently massage the marinade into the steak until completely coated, then seal the bag. Pop the bag into the fridge and leave for at least 1 hr, but up to 2 days is fine.

**STEP 2**

To cook, heat a heavy-based frying pan, griddle pan or barbecue until very hot. Wipe the excess marinade off the steak, then sear for 3 mins on each side for medium-rare or a few mins longer if you prefer the meat more cooked. Set aside for 1 min to rest. Carve the beef into thick slices and serve with a crunchy salad made with the spinach, cucumber, celery, radish and sesame seeds.

# Beef bulgogi stir-fry

**Prep:**10 mins **Cook:**10 mins

**Serves 4**

## Ingredients

- 4cm/1 ½in piece of ginger
- 4 tbsp soy sauce
- 4 tbsp mirin
- 3 garlic cloves
- 2 tbsp chopped pineapple
- 2 tsp red chilli flakes or Korean chilli powder
- 3 tbsp golden caster sugar
- 3 tsp sesame oil
- 500g sirloin or rump steak , trimmed of fat and sliced
- 1 large onion , cut into half moons
- 1 tbsp toasted sesame seeds
- 200g cooked basmati rice
- chopped spring onions , to serve

**Method**

## STEP 1

Put the ginger, soy, mirin, garlic, pineapple, chilli flakes, sugar and 1 tsp of the sesame oil in a food processor and blend until fine. Pour the marinade into a bowl, add the meat, mix well and leave to sit while you prepare the onion.

## STEP 2

Heat the remaining sesame oil in a large wok or frying pan until very hot. Add the onion and stir-fry for a few mins. Add the beef and the marinade, stirring constantly until it's cooked through, about 5 mins. Sprinkle with the sesame seeds and serve with rice and chopped spring onions.

# Beetroot & butternut stew

**Prep:**20 mins **Cook:**35 mins

**Serves 2**

# Ingredients

- 250g raw beetroot
- 350g butternut squash , unpeeled
- 1 garlic clove , grated
- 1 small onion , diced
- ¼ tsp cumin seeds
- ½ tsp ground coriander
- 4 cardamom pods , seeds removed and crushed
- 1 tbsp sunflower oil
- ½ tsp cinnamon
- 100g green beans , topped and cut in half
- 50g chard or spinach, stems removed and leaves roughly chopped
- small pack flat-leaf parsley , roughly chopped
- brown rice , to serve (optional)

**Method**

**STEP 1**

Peel the beetroot and chop into small pieces. Chop the butternut squash into small pieces. Put them in separate bowls until you need them.

### STEP 2

In a large wide-topped saucepan, fry the garlic, onion, cumin seeds, coriander and cardamom pods in the oil for 2 mins on a medium heat. Add 125ml water along with the beetroot and leave for a further 5 mins until the water has simmered away.

### STEP 3

Add 250ml water, the butternut squash and cinnamon, and leave to simmer on a medium heat for 10 mins. Add 250ml water and leave to simmer for another 10 mins.

### STEP 4

Add 125ml water, the green beans and simmer for another 5 mins until the water has simmered away. Take off the heat and stir in the chard and parsley. Serve by itself or with brown rice for a fuller meal.

# Thai cucumber slaw

**Prep:** 15 mins No cook

**Serves 4 - 6**

## Ingredients

- 2 spring onions , shredded
- zest and juice 1 lime
- 1 ½ tbsp fish sauce
- 2 tsp agave syrup
- 1 cucumber , cut into thin matchsticks
- 1 chinese leaf cabbage , finely sliced
- 1 red chilli , thinly sliced (optional)

### Method

### STEP 1

Fill a small bowl with cold water and add the spring onions, then set aside – this will make it curl. To make the dressing, combine the lime juice and zest, fish sauce and agave syrup.

## STEP 2

Toss together the cucumber, Chinese leaves and dressing, then transfer to a serving dish. Drain the spring onions and pat dry, then scatter over the slaw, and top with the chilli, if you like.

# BBQ salad pizza

**Prep:**25 mins **Cook:**20 mins Plus rising time

Serves 2-3

# Ingredients

### For the pizza dough

- strong white bread flour , plus extra for dusting
- ½ tsp easy or fast-action dried yeast

### For the topping

- 3 Little Gem lettuces , cut in half
- 6 spring onions
- 200g Tenderstem broccoli
- oil , for brushing
- 30g walnuts , toasted and roughly chopped

### For the dressing

- 75ml buttermilk (if you can't find any, squeeze a little lemon juice into milk and leave for 5 mins to sour)
- 2 tbsp thick Greek yogurt
- 1 tsp Dijon mustard
- ½ garlic clove , crushed
- 1 lemon , zested and juiced

**Method**

## STEP 1

To make the pizza dough, combine the flour, yeast and a big pinch of salt in a large bowl. Pour in 120ml warm water and knead together with well-floured hands to form a smooth dough. Put the dough back in its bowl, cover with a tea towel and leave somewhere warm to double in size. Can be made the night before and kept chilled overnight.

## STEP 2

For the buttermilk dressing, whisk together all the ingredients, adding lemon juice and some seasoning to taste. The dressing can be made the day before.

## STEP 3

Get your barbecue searingly hot. Brush the broccoli, spring onions and the cut side of the lettuce with a little oil, then put all the vegetables on the barbecue and cook until charred – broccoli will take the longest, between 8-10 mins. Have a plate ready so you can remove them when they're cooked.

## STEP 4

On a lightly floured surface, roll the pizza dough into a circle, about 30cm in diameter. Flour a large piece of foil, put the dough on top and carefully place on the barbecue. Put the lid on the barbecue and cook the dough, with the lid on throughout, for 6-8 mins, flipping halfway, or until cooked through – it may take slightly longer if your barbecue has lost some heat. Pile the charred veg on top of the dough, drizzle over some of the dressing (leaving some to dip the crusts), then scatter over the toasted walnuts and lemon zest to serve.

# Courgetti bolognese

**Prep:**15 mins **Cook:**1 hr

**Serves 4**

## Ingredients

- 2 tbsp olive oil
- 500g turkey mince (thigh or breast)
- 1 large onion , finely chopped
- 1 garlic clove , crushed
- 2 large carrots , peeled and diced
- 150g pack button mushrooms , roughly chopped
- 1 tbsp tomato purée
- 2 x 400g cans chopped tomatoes

- 2 chicken stock cubes
- 1 tbsp soy sauce
- 4 large courgettes
- grated pecorino or parmesan , to serve
- handful basil leaves

**Method**

**STEP 1**

Heat 1 tbsp of the olive oil in a large saucepan and add the turkey mince. Fry until browned, then scoop into a bowl and set aside.

**STEP 2**

Add the onion to the pan and cook on a low heat for 8-10 mins until tender. Then add the garlic, stirring for 1 min or so, followed by the carrot and the mushrooms, stirring for about 3 mins, until softened. Tip the turkey mince back into the pan, add the tomato purée, give everything a quick stir and tip in the chopped tomatoes. Fill 1 can with water and pour into the pan. Crumble over the chicken stock cubes and bring to the boil. Once boiling, lower the heat and simmer for about 1 hr, until the sauce has thickened and the veg is tender.

**STEP 3**

When the bolognese is nearly ready, stir through the soy sauce and some seasoning. Spiralize your courgettes on the large noodle attachment. Heat a large frying pan with the remaining 1 tbsp olive oil and add your courgetti. Cook until slightly softened, for 2-3 mins. Season with salt and serve topped with the turkey bolognese, grated pecorino and basil leaves.

# Lighter aubergine Parmigiana

**Prep:**35 mins **Cook:**55 mins

**Serves 4**

# Ingredients

- 2 tbsp rapeseed oil , plus 1 tsp
- 2 tbsp lemon juice

- 3 aubergines (750g/1lb 10oz total weight), stalk ends trimmed, cut into 1cm/1/2in lengthways slices
- 1 small onion , chopped
- 3 garlic cloves , finely chopped
- 400g can plum tomatoes
- 225g can plum tomatoes
- 1 tbsp tomato purée
- 2 tbsp chopped fresh oregano
- 100g ricotta
- 50g mozzarella , torn into small pieces
- handful basil leaves , roughly torn
- 2 medium tomatoes , sliced
- 25g vegetarian-style parmesan , grated

**Method**

**STEP 1**

Heat oven to 200C/180C fan/gas 6. Measure the 2 tbsp of oil into a small bowl. Brush just a little of it onto 2 large, non- stick baking sheets (if you only have 1 tray, bake the aubergines in batches). Mix the lemon juice into the measured oil. Lay the aubergine slices snugly in a single layer on the baking sheets, brush the tops with half the oil and lemon, season with pepper and bake for 20 mins. Turn the slices over, give the remaining oil and lemon mixture a good stir as it will have separated, and brush it over again. Season with pepper and bake for 10-15 mins more or until softened.

**STEP 2**

Meanwhile, heat the remaining 1 tsp oil in a medium saucepan. Add the onion and garlic and fry for 3-4 mins, stirring often, until the onion is softened and starting to brown. Tip in the cans of tomatoes, stir to break them up, then mix in the purée, pepper and a pinch of salt. Simmer uncovered for about 10-12 mins until thickened and saucy, then stir in the oregano.

**STEP 3**

Spread a little of the tomato sauce in the bottom of a shallow ovenproof dish (about 25 x 20 x 5cm). Start by laying a third of the aubergine slices widthways across the dish, spread over a third of the remaining sauce and put half the ricotta on top in small spoonfuls, then half the mozzarella. Scatter over half the torn basil and season well with pepper. Repeat the layering of aubergine slices, tomato sauce, ricotta, mozzarella and basil, and finish with the final aubergine slices, the sliced tomatoes and the last of the sauce. Season with pepper and scatter over the Parmesan. Bake for about 20 mins, or until the cheese is golden and the juices are bubbling.

# Yogurt parfaits with crushed strawberries & amaretti

**Prep:**10 mins **Serves 6**

## Ingredients

- 400g punnet strawberries , chopped
- 4 tbsp caster sugar
- 500g pot low-fat Greek yogurt
- 12 small amaretti biscuits , crushed

## Method

### STEP 1

In a small bowl, mix the strawberries with half the sugar, then roughly mash them with a fork so they are juicy. Mix the remaining sugar into the yogurt, then layer up 6 glasses with amaretti biscuits, yogurt and strawberries.

# Slow-cooker ham with sticky ginger glaze

**Prep:**20 mins **Cook:**7 hrs and 20 mins

**Serves 6 - 8**

## Ingredients

- 1 onion, thickly sliced
- 10 cloves, plus extra for studding
- 1 medium gammon joint, approx 1.3kg
- 1.5 litre bottle ginger beer
- 1 tbsp English mustard
- 3 tbsp ginger preserve

## Method

**STEP 1**

Put the onion and 10 cloves in the base of the slow cooker then nestle in the gammon joint. Pour over the ginger beer then cover and cook on LOW for 7 hours until the gammon is tender, but still holding its shape. You can cool then chill the gammon at this stage if you prefer.

**STEP 2**

Heat the oven to 200C/180C fan/ gas 6. Carefully remove the skin from the gammon leaving a layer of fat behind. Score the fat in a diamond pattern with a sharp knife, making sure you don't cut into the meat, then stud the centre of each diamond with cloves.

**STEP 3**

Mix the mustard and ginger preserve in a bowl, spoon or brush over the gammon then bake for 20 mins until golden and sticky. If roasting from cold you will need to add another 20 mins to the cooking time.

# Wild salmon with coconut chutney & green pilau

**Prep:** 15 mins **Cook:** 35 mins

**Serves 2**

## Ingredients

- 1 tsp rapeseed oil
- 1 onion , sliced
- 25g ginger , cut into thin matchsticks
- 2 garlic cloves , chopped
- 1 green chilli , deseeded and sliced
- ⅔ small pack coriander
- handful mint leaves
- 20g creamed coconut
- 1 lime , zested and 1/2 juiced
- 50g brown basmati rice
- 2 x 100g skinless wild salmon fillets , thawed if frozen
- head of spring greens (about 175g), stalks trimmed, finely shredded (remove outer leaves if tough)
- 125g frozen peas

- 1 tbsp ground coriander

**Method**

**STEP 1**

Heat oven to 200C/180C fan/ gas 6. Heat the oil in a large non-stick wok and add the onion, ginger, garlic and chilli. Cook briefly over a high heat to mix everything, then cover and leave to cook gently for about 10 mins until the onions are soft. Scoop two spoonfuls of the mixture into a bowl, add the coriander, mint, coconut, lime zest and juice with 1 tbsp water and blitz to a purée with a stick bender.

**STEP 2**

Meanwhile, boil the rice for 20 mins, then drain.

**STEP 3**

Spread half the coconut mixture over the fish and wrap up in a parcel of foil. Bake for 10 mins.

**STEP 4**

Carry on cooking the onions, uncovered this time, until they start to brown. Add the spring greens and stir-fry for a few mins until softened. Add the rice and peas with the ground coriander and cook until the veg is tender. If the mixture starts to stick, add 1 tbsp water. Stir through the remaining coconut mixture, then serve with the fish.

# Bean, ham & egg salad

**Prep:** 15 mins **Cook:** 15 mins

**Serves 4**

## Ingredients

- 2 eggs, hard-boiled
- 500g baby potato
- 200g green bean
- 200g frozen peas, defrosted
- 175g lean ham, shredded

**For the dressing**

- juice ½ lemon
- 1tbsp wholegrain mustard
- 1tbsp honey
- crusty bread, to serve (optional)

## Method

### STEP 1

Peel and quarter the eggs. Cook the potatoes in a large pan of boiling water for 8-10 mins or until tender. Tip in the beans for the final 3 mins, then add the peas for the final min. Drain all the veg, cool under cold running water, then drain really well.

### STEP 2

For the dressing, mix the juice, mustard and honey together. Season, then pour over the veg. Fold through the ham and top with the eggs. Serve with bread, if you like.

# Lemony mushroom pilaf

**Prep:**10 mins **Cook:**30 mins

**Serves 4**

## Ingredients

- 500ml vegetable stock
- 1 onion , sliced
- 300g mixed mushrooms , sliced
- 2 garlic cloves , crushed
- 200g mixed basmati rice and wild rice
- zest and juice 1 lemon
- small bunch snipped chives
- 6 tbsp light soft cheese with garlic and herbs

## Method

### STEP 1

Put 2 tbsp of the stock in a non-stick pan, then cook the onion for 5 mins until softened – add a splash more stock if it starts to dry out. Add mushrooms and garlic and cook for 2 mins more.

Add the rice and lemon zest and juice, mixing well. Pour in remaining stock and seasoning and bring to the boil. Turn down, cover and simmer for 25-30 mins until rice is tender. Stir through half each of the chives and soft cheese, then serve topped with the remaining chives and soft cheese.

# Ultimate toad-in-the-hole with caramelised onion gravy

**Prep:**20 mins **Cook:**40 mins plus 2 hrs resting

**Serves 4 - 6**

## Ingredients

- 140g plain flour
- 4 large eggs
- 300ml semi-skimmed milk
- 1 tbsp wholegrain mustard
- handful of woody herbs, leaves picked and chopped (we used 6 sage leaves, 4 rosemary sprigs and 4 thyme sprigs), plus a handful, fried until crispy, to serve (optional)
- 2 tbsp sunflower oil
- 8 rashers smoked streaky bacon
- 8 fat sausages (we used Cumberland but use your favourite variety)
- 2 red onions, cut into wedges
- cooked green vegetables (optional), to serve
- mash (optional), to serve

**For the gravy**

- drizzle of sunflower oil
- 2 red onions , halved and thinly sliced
- 1 tbsp golden caster sugar
- 2 tbsp balsamic vinegar
- 2 tbsp plain flour
- 250ml red wine
- 500ml chicken or beef stock

**Method**

**STEP 1**

Tip the flour into a large jug or bowl. Crack in the eggs, one at a time, whisking as you do. Pour in the milk and continue whisking until you have a smooth, lump-free batter. Add the mustard, herbs and some seasoning, then cover and set aside for 2 hrs, or chill overnight.

**STEP 2**

Heat oven to 220C/200C fan/gas 7. Heat the oil in a large metal roasting tin or enamel baking dish, roughly 30 x 22cm, with high-ish sides. Wrap a rasher of bacon around each sausage and pop them in the dish with the onion wedges. Place on the middle shelf of the oven (make sure the top shelf is removed to allow space for the batter to rise later). Cook for 15-20 mins until the sausages and bacon are browning and sizzling.

**STEP 3**

Meanwhile, make the gravy. Drizzle a little oil into a saucepan. Add the sliced onions and cook slowly for 15 mins. Stir every now and then until they are soft and caramelised. Add the sugar and balsamic vinegar, and cook for 5 mins more until sticky.

**STEP 4**

The batter should be the consistency of double cream - if it has become a little thick, add a splash of cold water. Take the batter to the oven, open the door, carefully pull out the shelf and quickly pour the batter around the sausages. Close the oven and do not open it again for at least 25 mins.

**STEP 5**

To finish the gravy, stir the flour into the onions to make a paste, cooking for 1-2 mins. Continue stirring while you splash in the wine, a little at a time, until you have a smooth, thick sauce. Increase the heat and bubble for a few mins until reduced by about half. Add the stock and some seasoning, and continue bubbling for 10 mins while the toad cooks.

**STEP 6**

By now the toad should be puffed up and deep golden brown. If not, continue cooking - but don't open the oven as it will sink. Serve scattered with the crisp herbs (if using), with the gravy, green veg, and mash, if you like.

# Turkey burgers with beetroot relish

**Prep:**15 mins **Cook:**10 mins

**Serves 4**

# Ingredients

- 500g pack turkey mince
- ½ tsp dried thyme or 2 tsp fresh
- 1 lemon

**For the relish**

- 250g cooked peeled beetroot (not in vinegar), finely diced
- 1 small red onion , finely chopped
- 2 tbsp chopped parsley
- 2 tsp olive oil
- 2 tsp wholegrain mustard
- Little Gem lettuce , to serve
- wholemeal pitta bread , to serve

**Method**

**STEP 1**

Tip turkey into a bowl with the thyme. Finely grate in the zest from the lemon and add a little seasoning. Use your hands to mix the ingredients well, then shape into 4 patties. Chill until ready to cook. Can be frozen for up to 1 month.

**STEP 2**

Mix the beetroot with the juice from ½ the lemon, onion, parsley, oil and mustard. Grill, griddle or barbecue the burgers for about 6 mins each side and serve with the beetroot relish, lettuce and pitta breads.

# Berry bake with passion fruit drizzle

**Prep:**15 mins **Cook:**30 mins

**Serves 6**

# Ingredients

- 100g/4oz low-fat spread
- 85g caster sugar
- grated zest and juice 1 lemon
- 1 egg
- 140g self-raising flour
- 1 tsp baking powder
- 4 tbsp low-fat natural yogurt , plus extra to serve (optional)
- 200g apple sauce
- 140g raspberries , blueberries or blackberries (or a mixture)
- 50g demerara sugar
- 2 passion fruits , halved and pulp scooped out

**Method**

**STEP 1**

Heat the oven to 180C/160C fan/gas 4. Lightly grease a medium baking dish with 1 tsp of the spread. Put the remaining spread, caster sugar, lemon zest, egg, flour, baking powder and yogurt in a mixing bowl. Whisk together for 2 mins until pale and fluffy. Stir in the apple sauce – this might make the mixture look curdled, but don't worry. Gently fold in the berries, then pour the batter into the prepared dish and level the surface. Bake for 25-30 mins until the sponge is golden brown and firm in the centre.

**STEP 2**

Meanwhile, mix lemon juice, demerara sugar and passion fruit pulp together. Remove pudding from the oven, lightly prick the surface with a fork and drizzle over passion fruit mixture. Serve warm with low-fat vanilla ice cream or the yogurt.

# Prawn & pak choi stir-fry

**Prep:**5 mins **Cook:**6 mins

**Serves 2**

## Ingredients

- 2 tbsp sesame oil
- 100g mangetout
- 1 carrot , finely sliced

- 200g pak choi , washed and sliced
- 2 spring onions , sliced on the diagonal
- 300g straight-to-wok egg noodles
- 150g cooked king prawns
- 2 tbsp soy sauce , plus extra to serve, (optional)
- 1 tbsp sesame seeds , toasted
- 1 red chilli , sliced, to serve (optional)

**Method**

**STEP 1**

Heat 1 tbsp sesame oil in a large wok or frying pan over a medium-high heat and toss in the mangetout and carrot. Cook for a few mins until starting to soften and brown, then add the pak choi and spring onions. Add the noodles and prawns, use tongs to combine, and warm through.

**STEP 2**

Pour in the soy sauce and remaining sesame oil, and toss to coat. Just before serving, scatter over the sesame seeds and chilli. Serve with extra soy sauce, if you like.

# Mushroom & chickpea burgers

**Prep:**10 mins **Cook:**20 mins

**Serves 4**

## Ingredients

- 1 tbsp olive oil
- 250g chestnut mushroom , finely chopped
- 2 garlic cloves , crushed
- 1 bunch spring onions , sliced
- 1 tbsp medium curry powder
- zest and juice ½ lemon
- 400g can chickpea , rinsed and drained
- 85g fresh wholemeal breadcrumb
- 6 tbsp 0% Greek yogurt
- pinch ground cumin

- 2 mixed-grain muffins or rolls, toasted and halved
- 2 plum tomatoes , sliced
- handful rocket leaves

## Method

### STEP 1

Heat 1 tsp oil in a non-stick frying pan and cook the mushroom, garlic and spring onion for 5 mins. Mix in the curry powder, lemon zest and juice and cook for 2 mins or until mixture looks quite dry. Tip out onto a plate to cool slightly.

### STEP 2

Use a potato masher or fork to mash the chickpeas in a bowl, leaving a few chunky pieces. Add the mushroom mix and the crumbs, then shape into 4 patties. Fry in the remaining oil for 3-4 mins on each side until crisp and browned.

### STEP 3

Mix the yogurt with the cumin. Place half a muffin on each plate, then spread with the yogurt. Top with the burgers, a few slices of tomato and a little rocket.

# Asian pulled chicken salad

**Prep:**20 mins No cook

**Serves 5**

## Ingredients

- 1 small roasted chicken , about 1kg
- ½ red cabbage , cored and finely sliced
- 3 carrots , coarsley grated or finely shredded
- 5 spring onions , finely sliced on the diagonal
- 2 red chillies , halved and thinly sliced
- small bunch coriander , roughly chopped, including stalks
- 2 heaped tbsp roasted salted peanuts , roughly crushed

**For the dressing**

- 3 ½ tbsp hoisin sauce

- 1 ½ tbsp toasted sesame oil

**Method**

**STEP 1**

Combine the dressing ingredients in a small bowl and set aside.

**STEP 2**

Remove all the meat from the chicken, shred into large chunks and pop in a large bowl. Add the cabbage, carrots, spring onions, chillies and half the coriander. Toss together with the dressing and pile onto a serving plate, then scatter over the remaining coriander and peanuts.

# Curtido

**Prep:**15 mins **Cook:**5 mins plus chilling

**Serves 4**

# Ingredients

- 1 small white cabbage (around 680g), finely shredded
- 1 red onion , finely sliced
- 2 carrots , thinly sliced lengthways
- 50ml apple cider vinegar
- 2 tsp golden caster sugar
- ½ small pack coriander , leaves only, roughly chopped

**Method**

**STEP 1**

Mix the cabbage with the onion and carrots in a heatproof bowl. Heat the vinegar, sugar and 1 tsp salt in a pan over a low heat until dissolved, then pour over the vegetables and mix well.

**STEP 2**

Put the slaw in the fridge for at least 30 mins or until ready to serve. Just before serving, stir through the coriander leaves and season well, to taste.

# Goat's cheese, tomato & olive triangles

**Prep:**5 mins No cook

**Serves 2**

# Ingredients

- 3 triangular bread thins
- 50g soft goat's cheese
- 2 x 5cm lengths of cucumber , thinly sliced lengthways
- 3 tomatoes , sliced
- 4 Kalamata olives , finely chopped
- 2 small handfuls rocket leaves

**Method**

**STEP 1**

Follow our triangular bread-thins recipe to make your own.

**STEP 2**

Cut the bread thins in half, put cut-side up and spread with the goat's cheese. Top with the cucumber and tomato, then scatter over the olives and top with the rocket. Eat straight away or pack into lunchboxes for later.

Printed in Great Britain
by Amazon